Elizabeth Lyons and Heather Peters

with contributions by
Chang Ch'eng-mei
Gregory Possehl

Published by

The University Museum
University of Pennsylvania
1985

This catalogue was produced in part through income provided by the Etelka J. Greenfield Publications Endowment.

Library of Congress Cataloging in Publication Data

Lyons, Elizabeth.
Buddhism : the history and diversity of a great tradition.
Bibliography: p. 62
1. Buddhism—History. I. Peters, Heather.
II. Title.
BQ266.L86 1985 294.3′09 85-28817
ISBN 0-934718-76-8

CONTENTS

ACKNOWLEDGMENTS

From the time of its founding nearly a century ago The University Museum has maintained an interest in the various regions of Asia. Early in its history the Museum acquired the unique collection of early Buddhist art housed in the Rotunda, as well as many items from modern times relating to the practice of Buddhism in a variety of countries.

Today Buddhism is a major world religion, 251 million strong, practiced not only in Asia but in Europe and the United States as well. In Philadelphia alone, the Asian community now numbers more than 90,000, many of whom are practicing Buddhists. Many of these individuals have recently arrived in our midst from Southeast Asia. Thus, there is an opportunity for The University Museum to encourage a better understanding of our new citizens and to help welcome them to our city through an exhibition showing both the history and diversity of Buddhism in Asia. To do so, we have arranged the exhibition both geographically and chronologically to give some indication of how Buddhism links the cultures of Asia while at the same time serves as a vehicle for expressing their separate cultural traditions.

A museum exhibition comes about only through the hard work of many individuals. First I would like to thank the co-curators, Dr. Heather Peters and Miss Elizabeth Lyons, without whose overriding direction and guidance this installation would not have been possible. They were fortunate to have the assistance of University of Pennsylvania students Chang Ch'eng-mei, Hilary Fraser and Elyssa Kane.

The exhibition also received valuable input from several scholars resident in various departments at the University of Pennsylvania. We gratefully acknowledge the time and advice freely offered by Dr. Guy Welbon of the Department of Religious Studies and Drs. Dale Saunders, Kenneth Kraft and Victor Mair of the Oriental Studies Department, who read sections of this handbook. We, of course, remain responsible for its final content.

The exhibition would not have materialized if it had not been for the creativity and hard work of the Exhibits Department under the direction of John T. Murray, ably assisted by Stephen Oliver, George Bucher, William Bucher, Tom Brown and Kathryn Grabowski. Without John Murray's artistic vision and guidance, the more than 130 artifacts on display here would not have been translated into a cohesive visual experience, nor would the spectacular re-created Japanese altar have become a reality. We would also like to express our grateful thanks to Maude de Schauensee, Keeper of the Museum's Near Eastern Section, for lending her drawing skills to create the beautifully executed reconstruction of the badly damaged Central Asian fresco on exhibit.

Among the others we would like to mention specifically are Dr. Koji Shimada, who introduced Heather Peters to the Japanese Buddhist community in Seabrook, New Jersey; Khun Narong of the Bangkok House and leader in the Philadelphia Thai-Lao Buddhist community; Dr. David A. Feingold of the Institute for the Study of Human Issues, for his Southeast Asian expertise; Khun Pisit Charaoenwongsa of the Thai Fine Arts Department, Thailand; and Khun Satharn Pairaoh without whose help the small collection of Thai amulets would not have been included.

We gratefully acknowledge The Institute for Museum Services for their generous museum conservation grant #IC-40044-84 which permitted us to carry out the conservation and restoration that was necessary for many of our objects. Virginia Greene, Christine Del Re, and Ann Heywood of the Museum's Conservation Department, with the assistance of Rosa Lowinger, private consultant, did a superb job of preparing the objects for exhibition. Many of the materials required extensive restoration, and the team experimented with interesting and innovative Japanese techniques. We would also like to thank The Phoebe W. Haas Charitable Foundation for enabling us to restore the fine Japanese Buddhist paintings displayed in the exhibition.

The Philadelphia Museum of Art also contributed to our exhibit by lending us certain pieces that filled important gaps in our installation. Our special thanks are extended to Miss Jean Lee, Curator of the Far Eastern Section, and Betsy Johnson of the South Asian Section for facilitating this loan.

During the planning of the exhibition we also received help from unexpected places. The magnificent Buddha which sits in the center of our re-created 19th century Japanese altar came to us through the generosity of Strawbridge and Clothier when they learned of our need for such a figure.

The photographic studio, with Harmer Fred Schoch as the chief photographer, produced most of the beautiful photographs used in both the exhibition and the handbook; these illustrations contribute to a deeper understanding of the material. Mary Anne Kenworthy, Photographic Archivist, lent her expertise by helping to locate existing photographs and by suggesting ones to use. The Publications Division, under the supervision of Barbara Murray, produced this fine handbook. Special thanks to Jennifer Quick for her patient editing expertise and to Martha Phillips for the beautiful layout and artistic design.

And finally, we would like to acknowledge the scores of friends, many from the Asian communities here in Philadelphia as well as abroad, who have offered advice, encouragement and fresh insight. Many are nameless, such as the numerous Buddhist monks and believers who generously shared their views with co-curator Heather Peters during her visits to China and Thailand in 1984 and 1985. So many took the time to explain, to listen or to comment. To all of them we say thank you.

Robert H. Dyson, Jr.
Director
The University Museum

INDIA: THE HISTORICAL FOUNDATIONS OF BUDDHISM

Introduction

Buddhism today is a world-wide religion embraced by millions. It is a complex system of beliefs, sometimes mystical in content, with scores of different sects. Diverse societies with long histories are intimately associated with Buddhism. Some 2500 years of Buddhist thought have yielded seemingly endless variations on the core of Buddhist belief. The iconography of this religion is a topic to which individual scholars have dedicated long and productive careers.

This introduction to the history and diversity of Buddhism and to the presentation of Buddhist materials in the collections of The University Museum is intended to familiarize the reader with the fundamentals of this tradition. It is the story of the foundings of Buddhism in ancient India and its subsequent diversification as it spread into China and Japan through the Silk Route and into the lands of Southeast Asia via sea-borne commerce and travel.

According to most scholars the historical Buddha, a man known as Siddhartha Gautama, probably was born about 560 B.C., but the earliest history of Buddhism is preserved only in the form of texts surviving from a considerably later age. Sculpted scenes from his life began systematically to appear in northwest India in the 2nd to 4th centuries A.D. This kind of historical circumstance demands that we be critical of our sources. We must keep in mind that both the story of the life of the Buddha and the accounts of his teachings we give here are taken from the beliefs of his later devotees, not from accurate, dispassionate accounts emanating directly from these events.

The story of the life of the historical Buddha tells us that he was born a prince of a noble Indian family living in the foothills of the Himalayas. The present place associated with Kapilavastu, the site of his birth, is Piprawa, which has been excavated recently by scholars from the Archaeological Survey of India. They found remains dating from the middle of the first millennium B.C., confirming at least that much of tradition. The story of his life as it comes to us from the Buddhist canon has been very finely rendered by Professor A.L. Basham in his book *The Wonder That Was India.* We have taken the following text from this source.

Large Buddha head of gray schist. Gandhara, India, 2nd to 3rd century A.D. H. 34 cm.

The Traditional Story of the Life of the Buddha

One night Mahamaya, chief queen of Suddhodhana, king of the Sakyas, dreamt that she was carried away to the divine lake Anavatapta in the Himalayas, where she was bathed by the heavenly guardians of the four quarters of the universe. A great white elephant holding a lotus flower in his trunk approached her, and entered her side. . . . Next day the dream was interpreted for her by wise men—she had conceived a wonderful son, who would be either a Universal Emperor . . . or a Universal Teacher. The child was born in a grove of sal trees called Lumbini, near the capital of the Sakyas, Kapilavastu, while his mother was on the way to her parents' home for her confinement. At birth he stood upright, took seven strides, and spoke: "This is my last birth—henceforth there is no more birth for me."

The boy was named Siddhartha, at a great ceremony on the fifth day from his birth. His *gotra* [clan] name was Gautama . . . by which he is commonly referred to in Buddhist literature. The soothsayers prophesied that he would become a Universal Emperor, with the exception of one, who declared that four signs would convince him of the misery of the world, and he would become a Universal Teacher. To prevent this prophecy coming true King Suddhodhana resolved that he should never know the sorrows of the world. He was reared in delightful palaces, from whose parks every sign of death, disease and misery was removed. He learned all the arts that a prince should learn, and excelled as a student. He married his cousin Yasodhara, whom he won at a great contest at which he performed feats of strength and skill. . . .

But for all his prosperity and success he was not inwardly happy, and for all the efforts of his father he did see the four signs foretold, which were to decide his career, for the gods knew his destiny, and it was they who placed the signs before him. One day, as he was driving round the royal park with his faithful charioteer Channa, he saw an aged man, in the last stages of infirmity and decrepitude—actually a god, who had taken this disguise in order that Siddhartha Gautama might become a Buddha. Siddhartha asked Channa who this repulsive being was, and when he learned that all men must grow old he was even more troubled in mind. This was the first sign. The second came a little later, in the same way, in the form of a very sick man, covered with boils and shivering with fever. The third was even more terrible—a corpse, being carried to the cremation-ground, followed by weeping mourners. But the fourth sign brought hope and consolation—a wandering religious beggar, clad in a simple yellow robe, peaceful and calm, with a mien of inward joy. On seeing him Siddhartha realized where his destiny lay, and set his heart on becoming a wanderer.

Sandstone head of the Buddha from Mathura, India. Late 1st to early 3rd century A.D. H. 22.86 cm., W. 16.51 cm.

Hearing of this King Suddhodhana doubled his precautions. Siddhartha was made a virtual prisoner, though still surrounded with pleasures and luxuries of all kinds; his heart knew no peace, and he could never forget the four signs. One morning the news was brought to him that Yasodhara had given birth to a son, but it gave him no pleasure. That night there were great festivities, but when all were sleeping, he roused Channa, who saddled his favourite horse Kanthaka, and he rode off into the night, surrounded by rejoicing demigods, who cushioned the fall of his horse's hoofs so that no one should hear his departure. . . .

When far from the city he stripped off his jewellery and fine garments and put on a hermit's robe, provided by an attendant demigod. . . . Thus Siddhartha performed his "Great Going Forth" . . . and became a wandering ascetic, owning nothing but the robe he wore.

At first, he begged his food as a wanderer, but he soon gave up this life for that of a forest hermit. From a sage named Alara Kalama he learned the technique of meditation, and the lore of Brahman as taught in the Upanisads; but he was not convinced that man could obtain liberation from sorrow by self-discipline and knowledge, so he joined forces with five ascetics who were practising the most rigorous self-mortification in the hope of wearing away their karma and obtaining final bliss.

His penances became so severe that the five quickly recognised him as their leader. For six years he tortured himself until he was nothing but a walking skeleton. One day, worn out by penance and hunger, he fainted, and his followers believed that he was dead. But after a while he recovered consciousness, and realized that his fasts and penances had been useless. He again began to beg food, and his body regained its strength. The five disciples left him in disgust at his backsliding.

One day Siddhartha Gautama, now thirty-five years old, was seated beneath a large pipal tree on the outskirts of the town of Gaya, in the realm of Bimbisara king of Magadha. Sujata, the daughter of a nearby farmer, brought him a large bowl of rice boiled in milk. After eating some of this he bathed, and that evening, again sitting beneath the pipal tree, he made a solemn vow that, though his bones wasted away and his blood dried up, he would not leave his seat until the riddle of suffering was solved.

So for forty-nine days he sat beneath the tree. At first he was surrounded by hosts of gods and spirits, awaiting the great moment of enlightenment; but they soon fled, for Mara, the spirit of the world and of sensual pleasure, the Buddhist devil, approached. For days Gautama withstood temptations of all kinds. . . .

At last the demon hosts gave up the struggle and Gautama, left alone, sank deeper and deeper into meditation. At the dawning of the forty-ninth day he knew the truth. He had found the secret of sorrow, and understood at last why the world is full of suffering and unhappiness of all kinds, and what man must do to overcome them. He was fully enlightened—a Buddha. For another seven weeks he remained under the Tree of Wisdom (*bodhi*), meditating on the great truths he had found. . . . Leaving the Tree of Wisdom, he journeyed to the Deer Park near Varanasi (the modern Sarnath), where his five former disciples had settled to continue their penances.

To these five ascetics the Buddha preached his first sermon, or, in Buddhist phraseology, "set in motion the Wheel of the Law". The five were so impressed with his new doctrine that they gave up their austerities and once more became his disciples. A few days later a band of sixty young ascetics became his followers, and he sent them out in all directions to preach the Buddhist

Dharma [doctrine]. Soon his name was well known throughout the Ganga Plain, and the greatest kings of the time favoured him and his followers. He gathered together a disciplined body of monks (called *bhiksus*. . . . literally "beggers"), knit together by a common garb, the yellow robes of the order, and a common discipline, according to tradition laid down in detail by the Buddha himself. . . .

For eight months of the year the Buddha and his followers would travel from place to place, preaching to all and sundry. For the four months of the rainy season, roughly corresponding to the English summer, they would stop in one of the parks given to the Buddhist order by wealthy lay followers, living in huts of bamboo and reed—the first form of the great Buddhist monasteries of later times. For over forty years his reputation grew and the Sangha (literally Society, the Buddhist Order) increased in numbers and influence . . . His ministry was a long, calm and peaceful one. . . .

The end came at the age of eighty. He spent the last rainy season of his life near the city of Vaisali, and after the rains he and his followers journeyed northwards to the hill country which had been the home of his youth. On the way he prepared his disciples for his death. He told them that his body was now like a worn-out cart, creaking at every joint. He declared that he had made no distinction between esoteric and exoteric teaching, but had preached the full doctrine to them. When he was gone they were to look for no new leader—the Doctrine (*Dharma*) which he had preached would lead them. They must rely on themselves, be their own lamps, and look for no refuge outside themselves.

At the town of Pava he was entertained by a lay disciple, Cunda the smith, and ate a meal of pork. Soon after this he was attacked by dysentery, but he insisted on moving on to the nearby town of Kusinagara. . . . Here, on the outskirts of the town, he lay down under a sal tree, and that night he died. His last words were: "All composite things decay. Strive diligently!" This was his "Final Blowing-Out". . . . His sorrowing disciples cremated his body, and his ashes were divided between the representatives of various tribal peoples and King Ajatasatru of Magadha.

The Teachings of the Buddha

Thus, Siddhartha Gautama was very much a part of his own culture when he set out for the plains and forests of the Ganges Valley. It seems reasonable for us to believe that initially, at least, his quest was a personal one, that he was seeking his own salvation, not the foundation of an institution or the creation of a religion. Some scholars even suspect that the *Sangha,* the Community of Monks, grew slowly because of his reluctance to proselytize. In the end, he laid down some rules of conduct for the Sangha and allowed some of the monks to accompany him on his seasonal trek through north India. These rules were probably very much like the "Ten Precepts" of the modern Buddhist order: an acceptance to refrain from 1) harming living things, 2) taking what is not given, 3) evil behavior in passion, 4) false speech, 5) alcoholic drinks, 6) eating at forbidden times, 7) dancing, singing, music and dramatic performances, 8) the use of garlands, perfumes, unguents and jewelry, 9) the use of a high or broad bed, and 10) receiving gold and silver.

Siddhartha Gautama sought Nirvana, a highly refined stage of enlightenment. (Nirvana is a concept that was accepted by adherents of various religions of the time.) His great transformation from ordinary mortal to the Buddha marked his achievement of this state. It would be wrong to think of Nirvana only as a mental condition of happiness, or as simple intellectual insight and knowledge of the world, society, religion or philosophy. The achievement of Nirvana marks an end to the cycle of rebirth for those who attain it. Nirvana is neither a state of being nor is it a state of non-being. Nirvana is not of this universe. It is enduring, permanent, a secure shelter, unassailable bliss. It is the supreme Truth and Reality. Nirvana is the only thing that is truly worthwhile. Nirvana underlies everything, but is not a part of it. One needs to relax the habitual constraints of western logic to even begin to deal with this concept. A state of neither being nor non-being suggests a third state—Nirvana. This is the true release from a crass physical world, one ruled by such "trivia" as Aristotelian logic and the methods of science.

Stela depicting the Eight Miracles of the Buddha. India, Pala period (8th to 12th century A.D.). H. 59.53 cm., W. 50.28 cm.

Gandharan stone frieze showing three scenes of Buddha with attendants. India, 2nd century A.D. L. 60.96 cm., H. 16.51 cm.

Buddhism affirms what it calls the "Three Jewels." The Buddha himself is the first. The *Dharma* (doctrine) and Sangha are the second and the third. Dharma is at once the Truth and the content of the Buddha's teaching. It was the Dharma, tradition tells us, that the enlightened Buddha preached in the Deer Park at Sarnath. This sermon introduced the Buddha's Middle Path: the rejection of both the extremes of asceticism, as well as the coarse material world. He also brought forth the core of his doctrine in the form of the "Four Noble Truths": There is no existence without suffering. The cause of suffering is egocentric desire. The end of suffering is achieved through the elimination of desire. The Noble Eightfold Path is the way to eliminate desire. These eight principles are: 1) Correct View, 2) Correct Mental Attitude, 3) Correct Speech, 4) Correct Action, 5) Correct Pursuits, 6) Correct Effort, 7) Correct Mindfulness, 8) Correct Contemplation.

The insights of the living Buddha were powerful, and his compelling message attracted adherents. There were, however, other men who also sought to be enlightened teachers of the day in this era of Indian history, such as Mahavira, the founder of Jainism, and teachers of a doctrine associated with modern Hinduism.

Cultural, Historical Context of Early Buddhism

The Aryan civilization and thought provide an important foundation for the later development of Buddhism. According to current research, the Aryans can best be understood as immigrants from a region to the north, in what is now the Soviet Union. During the second millennium B.C., small groups of these people moved into South Asia. They were a nomadic and horse riding people whose subsistence was based on cattle pastoralism, with some crop cultivation.

The Vedas, a body of four religious texts composed in Sanskrit by the Aryans, are the oldest historical records in India and Pakistan and contain elements of non-Aryan beliefs associated with the cultural traditions of indigenous Indian peoples. (Sanskrit is an Indo-European tongue, related to Latin, Greek, ancient Persian and other languages. Many of the modern languages of northern India and Pakistan, such as Hindi, are derived from it.) These texts were brought together and finally codified as a sacred document between about 1200 and 800 B.C.

The Vedas were primarily concerned with the proper conduct of the Aryan animal sacrifice and were later expanded upon in a massive set of religious texts we call the Brahmanas, Aryanakas and Upanishads. The Brahmanas seem to belong to a period slightly later than that of the Vedas, approximately 800 to 600 B.C., and the earliest Upandishads are only slightly older than the birth date of Siddhartha Gautama.

These later texts enlarge upon the ideas of the Vedas, at times in a most critical way. They reflect and justify a revision of the older Aryan social order and lay the foundation for what we see today as the earliest tendencies toward the distinctly Indian caste structure. Much of the speculative thought that fueled these changes was conducted by learned ascetics who taught on the outskirts of the villages and towns of the Ganges Valley. One of these men was the Buddha.

Thus, many of the most fundamental Buddhist teachings come to us as a set of ideas shared with other systems of belief. Buddhists did not create the idea of Nirvana. This concept was very much a part of the historical thought of the times of Siddhartha Gautama. Moreover, the Buddha's concern with the transmigration of souls is also something that is shared with other Indian religions.

Buddhism differs from most contemporary sectarian developments in north India of the 5th and 6th

(Continued on page 17)

Opposite
Standing Buddha. Gray schist. Gandhara, India, 2nd century A.D. H. 113.5 cm.

page 10
L. *Fugen, the bodhisattva who embodies goodness and protects devotees of the* Lotus Sutra, *rides a white elephant. Wood with lacquer, paint and gilt.* R. *Monju, the bodhisattva of wisdom and guardian of the sacred doctrine, sits upon a lion holding his attributes of sword and scroll. Wood with paint and gilt. Japan, 19th century. H. (Monju) 57 cm., W. 38 cm.*

page 11
Shotoku Taishi, a 6th century regent and ardent supporter of Buddhism, depicted as a child. Japan, Kamakura period (A.D. 1185–1333). Wood with traces of paint. H. 106.5 cm.

page 12
Fudo is the fiercest of the Myo-o, the deities who combat evil. Japan, 19th century. Wood with black, red and gold lacquer. H. 144.78 cm., W. 83.82 cm.

page 13
Life-sized figure of a seated Patriarch or monk. Japan, 19th century. Wood, paint and lacquer. H. 84 cm.

page 14
Embroidered Kakemono (hanging scroll) depicting the death of Sakyamuni. The paper was painted, then embroidered; the Buddha is done with coiled gold thread, other figures with silk. Japan, 17th to 18th century. L. 192.5 cm., W. 117 cm.

page 15
Butsudan. Large household shrine containing a standing figure of Amida Buddha. Wood lacquered black and trimmed with brass; interior gilded. Japan, 19th century. H. 84 cm., W. at base 71 cm.

page 16
Small portable shrine with figure of Aizen Myo-o. Japan, 19th century. Wood lacquered black and decorated with brass; gilded interior. H. 27.94 cm., W. 18.41 cm.

centuries B.C. in the focus of its central concern—the release of the mortal soul from the cycle of rebirth. Belief in the existence of a god or gods (theism) is also not of primary importance for all Buddhists. In general, the highest, most refined thoughts offered by Buddhist teachers and philosophers reveal a lack of concern for external gods. If pressed they will assert the supremacy of the Buddha over any of the gods one might name: Brahma, Vishnu, Shiva and the like. But there is a certain indifference to a creator god. After all, what have gods got to do with finding release from suffering? On the other hand, if one moves to the village almost anywhere in Asia, one can find a great deal of Buddhist concern with gods of many forms and persuasions: Buddhist, Hindu, animistic, even Christian. Thus, while theism is present, it does not seem to play the central role in early Buddhism that it does in the other religions of that time.

Early Buddhist Iconography and Practice

After the Buddha died at Kushinagara around 480 B.C. his cremated ashes, and apparently some charred bone and teeth, were divided among the devout as remembrances of him. According to tradition, these remains were taken to various parts of northern India and buried or otherwise interred under *stupas* (burial mounds). These were initially small, but later became quite monumental in scale.

The stupas, which became important places of worship and pilgrimage for Buddhists, are also a key element in the Buddhist cult of the *caitya* or sacred location. One part of mid to late first millennium B.C. north Indian belief accepted that certain locations were the abode of special spirits, or were places with particular power. These caityas might be groves of trees, the burial tumuli of chiefs, or even large rocks in open fields, cascading water or any spot of unusual property. The Buddhists took over the notion of the caitya and developed it to their particular end.

The historical Buddha had recommended that monks travel for all of the year, save for the monsoon season. But following his death, monks in increasing numbers settled on the outskirts of villages and towns to beg, teach and proselytize. They chose the local caityas as appropriate abodes for monks, and over time these became small monasteries. This process took many years, even generations. Yet it was important since it advanced the institutionalization of Buddhism as a religion. This had begun when the historical Buddha allowed followers to gather around and accompany him on his yearly migration. It was furthered when he established rules for the monks who would follow him. The construction of permanent facilities was yet another step in this direction.

Especially important in this caitya cult were places of significance in the life of the Buddha: the Lumbini Grove at Kapilavastu, Siddhartha's birthpiace; the *bodhi* "Tree of Enlightenment" in Gaya; the Deer Park at Sarnath where he first preached; Kushinagara where he died. Each of these places was associated with an iconographic element that would recall the Buddha. The bodhi tree symbolized his enlightenment, the deer recalled his ministry and the stupa his death. In the early decades following his "Final Blowing Out," the image of the Buddha was not rendered. It was instead these elements that symbolized him. Other elements, such as the *Buddhapada,* the footprints of the Buddha, were also used to indicate his presence.

Final Institutionalization of Buddhism

As Buddhism grew and changed so too did the political institutions of India. The first great empire is associated with the Mauryan dynasty (c. 322–183 B.C.) of modern-day Bihar. The founder of this dynasty was a king known as Chandragupta (reigned c. 322–298 B.C.). Chandragupta's grandson Ashoka (269–232 B.C.) seems to have expanded Mauryan political influence over much of the subcontinent. It may be that he did not actually conquer and rule so vast an area, but his edicts, in the form of rock inscriptions and pillars, are extremely widespread.

According to Buddhist tradition, Ashoka, moved to remorse and pity by the horrors of war, came to the conclusion that true power was realized through religion not force. He, thus, became an active patron of Buddhism. Historical sources do support that Ashoka at least was influenced by Buddhism and that he supported the Sangha, establishing important precedents for later kings in Southeast Asia.

The political might of the Mauryans, as well as their patronage, brought the full institutionalization of Buddhism to reality. A hierarchy of offices was established, although there is no Buddhist "Pope." Vast numbers of monks occupied the monasteries which acquired property, at times large amounts of it, to support themselves and help the poor. The canon was expanded, diversified and refined. Sectarian movements flourished. The search for personal salvation by one man had became a vast apparatus, involving millions of people, supported by one of the ancient world's greatest empires.

The Stupa

We can presume that all, or nearly all, of the Buddha's cremated remains, which had been redistributed by Ashoka, were interred in stupas. All but one of the stupas of the Mauryan age, or slightly later, have been so extensively rebuilt that little remains to recall their original configurations. The most remarkable of these were at Bharhut, Sanchi and Amaravati

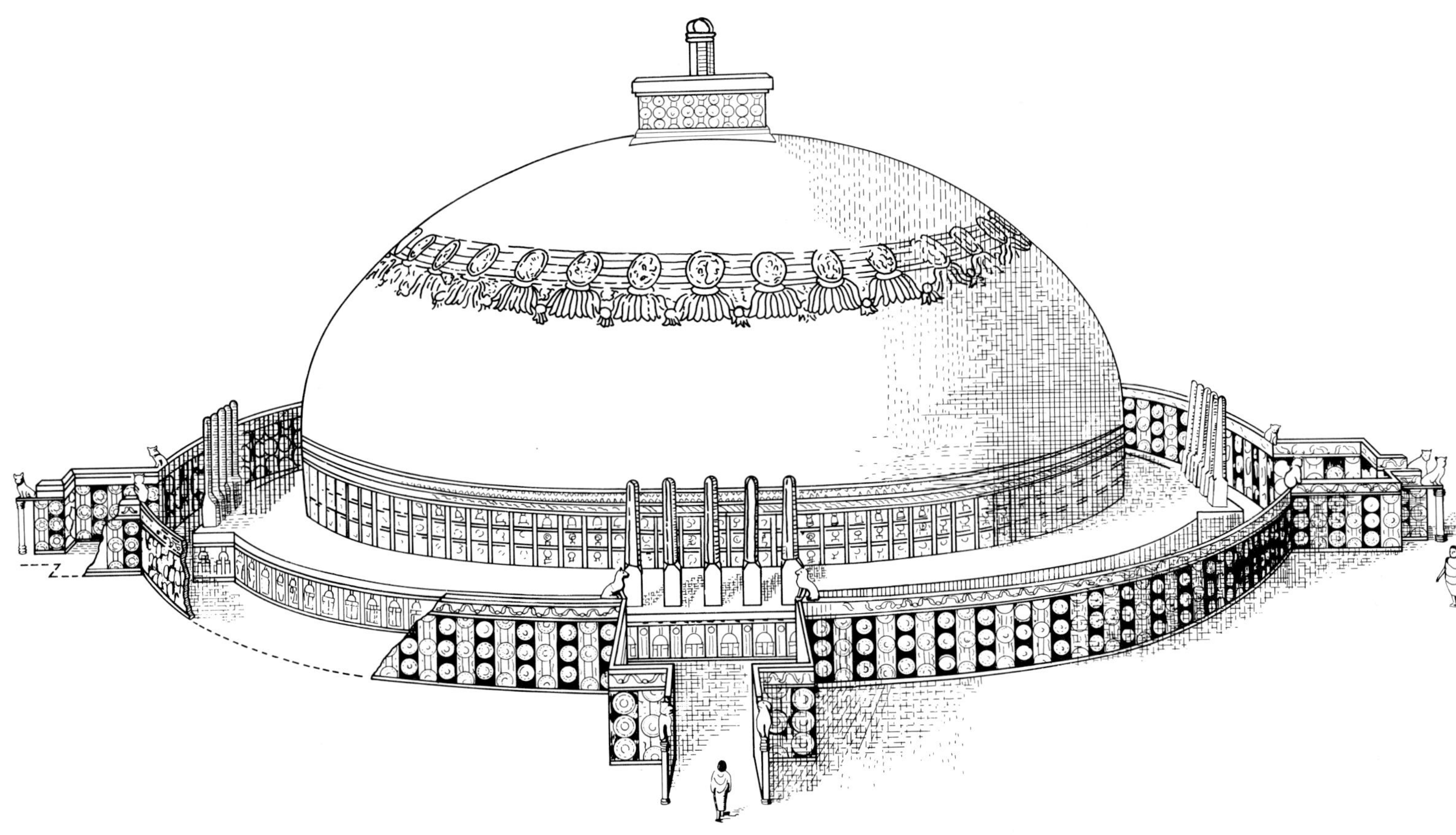

Reconstruction of the Great Stupa at Amaravati, India, ca. 1st to 2nd century A.D. (After M. Ricketts, Sculpture from Amaravati in the British Museum *by Douglas Barrett, 1954.)*

(see above). These stupas are large hemispheres surrounded by a railing, and the gateways are oriented to the cardinal directions. The principal form of worship at the stupa involved circling around it in the auspicious clockwise direction. The railings and gateways, along with the moldings of the stupa drum, were beautifully carved (see page 19). Themes varied from rosettes and other straightforward plant and animal motifs to elaborate scenes from the life of the historical Buddha or the many tales and stories associated with Buddhism.

In the center of the stupa is a small chamber with relics of, or recalling, the Buddha. At the stupa site of Devnimori in Gujarat, there is reasonable evidence that one of the relic caskets contains the actual ashes of the Buddha himself. But the more common finds are inscribed plaques or objects of precious and semiprecious stone and metal.

Associated with the stupa were monastic buildings, kitchens and hostels. In many instances, complexes of stupas and such associated facilities grew up. This is well illustrated at the Deer Park at Sarnath, which has an Ashokan edict, his stupa and a host of other buildings and stupas dating from this era and later ages.

The location of such early Buddhist establishments was guided by recollections of the Buddha's life, the location of caityas and to a remarkable degree by the trade routes of the day. Monasteries and crossroads seemed to coincide. We see this as relating to the initial spread of the religion under state patronage. Many of the routes the wandering monks followed must also have been the routes of commerce. We know that monks often traveled in the company of traders, spreading Buddhist beliefs as the traders spread their goods. Since Buddhists enjoyed the protection of the state, traders associating with them would have come under this protective umbrella. The monasteries were safe havens, used by ancient traders as way stations and halting spots in their travels. Their wealth came back to the monasteries in various forms of patronage and practical support.

This symbiosis between monks and traders was extremely important in the history of Buddhism. It was ultimately the agency that took this religion out of India and into China, Japan and Southeast Asia.

Fragment of the stupa railing from the Great Stupa at Amaravati, India. Rosette from a crossbar. 2nd century A.D. H. 71.12 cm., W. 76.20 cm.

Conservative Buddhism

To his followers, the historical Buddha was not a supernatural entity or deity. He was a mortal who had achieved a state of breathtaking brilliance, of cosmic proportions. His eminence was, in fact, greater than any god's. He was the greatest of teachers. He preached that a rebirth in heaven awaited those with faith and love for him. Not everyone had to strive for Nirvana immediately. We know that this prospect of a rebirth in heaven was more intelligible, and possibly more attractive, to the average person in ancient India than was the rather abstract notion of Nirvana.

The Buddha also taught that he was but the latest of a number of Buddhas who had preceded him over the ages. The conservative Theravada sect, which survives today in Sri Lanka and Southeast Asia, counted at least 25 such previous Buddhas.

Just prior to his death, the Buddha is said to have told his followers to look to the doctrine for guidance. His teachings were aimed at the salvation of individuals through an individual's personal struggle with reality and truth. Teachers could assist in this struggle, but it was up to the individual to achieve the indescribable Nirvana, which transformed them into *arhats,* the "Worthy." This key element in Buddhism changed as schism beset the religion, and its doctrine became more worldly.

Left on their own his followers brought about a number of important changes to the presumed literal interpretation of the Buddha's thought. For example, they settled into year-round abodes, forsaking the seasonal trek the Buddha himself undertook. They also accumulated property, at times in substantial quantity. However, a body of teaching, interpretation and accumulated knowledge remained that today can be seen as relatively conservative and orthodox, as compared to other aspects of sectarian Buddhism.

The long Buddhist tradition of Sri Lanka tells us that the orthodox Pali (the canonical language of Theravada Buddhism) canon of the Theravadans was written down during the reign of the King Vattagamani (89–77 B.C.); this sect is the predominant one today in both Sri Lanka and Southeast Asia. Conservative Buddhism is sometimes referred to as the "Lesser Vehicle" or *Hinayana* Buddhism. A more contemporary rendering of this sect is *Theravada* Buddhism. Conservative Buddhists find the term "Hinayana" offensive, since it contrasts their system of beliefs to something called *Mahayana* or the "Great Vehicle," which developed after orthodoxy had been largely defined. This is the principal reason that "Hinayana" is not used here.

The Spread of Theravada Buddhism to the East

Just as Buddhist orthodoxy was being fully defined, we find traces of this belief system emerging in Southeast Asia. Documentary sources and a reading of the archaeological record demonstrate that sea trade at about the time of Christ was the principal mechanism for this diffusion. Buddhist monks, as well as their Hindu and Jain contemporaries, were taking passage on trading ships moving to the east. They proselytized along the way, establishing more or less permanent settlements in Burma, Thailand and Cambodia. Excavated remains of this era document their settlements, and the material remains demonstrate an Indian connection.

The development of the Mahayana school in the northwest of the Indian subcontinent, well inland, led to other developments in the diffusion of Buddhism. It is to a consideration of these matters that we now turn.

Mahayana Buddhism in Northwestern India and Pakistan

The development of the Mahayana schools took place in the northern and western parts of the subcontinent from about the 2nd century B.C. to the 2nd and 3rd centuries A.D. The political history of Afghanistan, northern Pakistan and northwestern India in these times is extraordinarily complex. Greeks, the Parthian dynasty of Iran and Central Asians of several origins were in a constant tug of war over the region. In the end a dynasty known as the Kushana established itself in the first century A.D. and settled in for a relatively long period of political stability. The Kushana dynasty's greatest king, Kanishka (reigned c. A.D. 78–101), was a supporter of Buddhism and furthered the development of the Mahayana school of Buddhism.

During the centuries just before and after the birth of Christ, trade between China and the Mediterranean moved overland along what is called the Silk Route. Merchants from China, Central Asia, Pakistan, Afghanistan, India, Iran and the Mediterranean brought silks and other merchandise from China to Rome to exchange for Roman gold, furs, jade, fine horses and other wares. We know from texts, and from the archaeological record, that Buddhist monks accompanied Silk Route traders on their passage, especially to the east into China. The record of this progression is particularly strong in the westernmost reaches of China, in places like Xinjiang. Just as the spread of Buddhism to Southeast Asia was tied to trade, so too did China and ultimately Japan receive this message from proselytizing monks following the course of commerce. The Silk Route passed through the northwestern parts of the subcontinent; thus, Chinese and Japanese Buddhists are practitioners of the Mahayana sect, rather than the more orthodox Theravadan form.

Head of a mustached bodhisattva made of gray schist. Gandhara, India, 2nd century A.D. H. 25.4 cm., W. 16.51 cm.

Mahayana Buddhism as defined in the *Lotus Sutra* (a fundamental Mahayana text which stresses salvation for all people) can be seen in part as a logical development of earlier orthodoxy. This sect took the notion of the bodhisattva and developed it into a broad pantheon and an associated rich new mythology.

A bodhisattva refers to an enlightened being on his way to Buddhahood but who postpones his goal to keep a vow to help all life attain salvation. The Buddha was a bodhisattva in his earlier lives. The bodhisattva's creed includes good behavior, insight, power, wisdom in knowing how and when to act for the good of man, courage, charity and the like. Bodhisattvas may materialize as men, even animals, or they may remain more spiritual in character. Avalokitesvara, who embodies compassion, is a form of bodhisattva.

In many contexts there is an element of suffering in the bodhisattva's good works. Constant vigilance, even taking man's suffering as their own, can be documented in Mahayana doctrine. Mahayanists came to believe that it was somewhat self-centered, even selfish for men to seek Nirvana acting as individuals for their personal release from suffering. This is, of course, a significant break with orthodoxy. It is also a more or less logical outgrowth of the development of the cult of bodhisattvas and their humanistic work for all living things. Men should reject the arhat principle and instead strive to assist all living beings in the release from suffering. The Mahayanists refined the notion of "merit" as good deeds that could be transferred to others. Men could do more than teach and advise in the search for perfection. They could directly intercede on behalf of others and their search for release. Individuals should seek to become bodhisattvas.

The Mahayana doctrine also includes elements that have a wider popular appeal. For example, the broad pantheon of bodhisattvas is attractive and filled with festive life. The shift from a rigorous, difficult to understand search for personal salvation to one that finds fulfillment in group practice and sharing is also seductive. In fact, while Mahayana doctrine recognizes the Four Noble Truths, and the central role of the Buddhist notion of suffering in them, the sect is fundamentally optimistic. There is help for all who seek it. The Buddha's promise of a rebirth in heaven is there for all who will seek it. Ultimately, Mahayanists hold that all living entities are in some way bodhisattvas, and all life will ultimately reach Nirvana.

Of central importance to the Mahayanists is their development of a doctrine that holds that the historical Buddha had not been a man like the rest of us. Rather, he had been the earthly expression of a powerful spiritual entity with three aspects, or "Bodies": a Body of Essence, of Bliss and a Created Body. The Body of Essence pervades all and is the ultimate Buddha, sharing much with the notion of his achievement of Nirvana. There is an ethereal quality to the Body of Essence. The Body of Bliss, on the other hand, is more real. This aspect of the great Mahayana spirit lives in heavenly contentment, maintaining an awareness of both his heaven and our world. The Created Body is the earthly manifestation of this great spirit in the form of the historical Buddha.

GP

BUDDHISM IN CENTRAL ASIA

Two wall painting fragments of bodhisattvas. Probably from Turfan, Tang period (7–10th century A.D.). H. 27.95 cm.

Central Asia is a region comprised of parts of what today are northwestern Tibet, eastern Turkestan, northern Kashmir, northern Afghanistan and neighboring sections of the USSR. As noted above, Buddhism was first imported here from the northwest of the Indian subcontinent.

There were caravan routes in this region, linking oases on the north and south borders of the Taklamakan desert, in Xinjiang, that were used by tradesmen and pilgrims. One set of routes linked China and India, the second Iran and the Mediterranean world. The routes that linked China and India brought Chinese silks to the west and Indian Buddhism to China. It is the presence of these so-called Silk Routes that accounts for the strongly international flavor of the art, and especially the Buddhist art, of Central Asia.

Buddhism's history in Central Asia is but one of many cultural heritages. Iranian speaking peoples such as the Khotanese and the Sogdians, Turkish ethnic groups such as the Uighurs, as well as Tocharians and other groups all accepted Buddhism and left their mark upon it. From time to time the territory along both branches of the Silk Route in the eastern section of Central Asia was ruled by the Chinese. It was through contact with Central Asian Buddhist communities that China first came to know of the Indian religion. This has had a profound effect on the nature and development of Buddhism in China and elsewhere in East Asia.

After the Kushana empire fell in the late 3rd century A.D., local kingships grew up, but Indian influence, including that of Buddhism, remained strong. In the late 4th century a major disruption occurred in kingdoms in Chinese (eastern) Turkestan. Tibetan expansionism in Central Asia also led to a certain amount of political dislocation in areas ranging from Dunhuang to Khotan. Buddhism, however, continued to thrive through all of these vicissitudes. It was not until the coming of Islam to Central Asia in the middle of the 8th century A.D. that Buddhism's influence there began to dwindle. Henceforth, China would take a more active role in the formation and propagation of Buddhist doctrine.

BUDDHISM IN CHINA

Stone stela illustrating scenes from the Lotus and Vimalakirti sutras. China, A.D. 575. H. 2.13 m.

Introduction

According to legend, the Han Emperor Ming (r. A.D. 58–75) dreamed that a divine being appeared to him in the form of a "golden man." After he was informed that the "golden man" was in fact the Buddha, a divinity worshipped in India, the emperor dispatched an envoy to India. The envoy returned accompanied by Indian monks, a white horse bearing a sutra, and a golden image of the Buddha. In their honor, the Emperor allegedly established the White Horse Monastery (Bai Ma Si) which still exists today outside Luoyang, the capital at that time. (The present buildings date to the 14th–15th centuries A.D.)

Although reliable historical sources document that Buddhism had reached China and was known in imperial circles by the 1st century A.D., its entry was less dramatic than the colorful white-horse legend. It probably entered China via the early trade routes. Two major trade routes already existed by the Han period (206 B.C.–A.D. 220). The first was the northern land route, or Silk Route described above, which linked northern India with the Han Chinese capital via the Central Asian kingdoms of Kashgar, Kucha, Turfan and Khotan. The second, a southern sea route, linked South India with Canton via Southeast Asia.

The northern route via Central Asia played the more dominant and influential role. As we learned above, the Central Asian kingdoms were early recipients of both Indian and Chinese influences since these centers served as important transit points along the trade route. The Buddhist pilgrims who traveled along this route attached themselves to the caravans of the traders, and the various centers that served as important rest stops for the traders also became important Buddhist centers.

Thus, during the early centuries A.D. Buddhism gradually filtered into China, and its existence was acknowledged by both elite and popular society. However, Buddhism was not immediately embraced in China. Confucian philosophy, already dominant in the Han period, demanded strong state control, extolled the value of the family and the continuity of descendants, and stressed the practical and economic usefulness of Chinese citizens. Buddhism, on the other hand, required that an individual leave his family and remain celibate; Buddhist monks futhermore lived in the Sangha, or monastic community, whose self-declared autonomy threatened the centralized authority of the state, and monks traditionally subsisted on food and other donations provided by a pious laity. As early as the 3rd century A.D. literary evidence appeared documenting these intrinsic conflicts between Buddhism and traditional Confucian Chinese culture. The nature of the debates attacking and defending Buddhism have remained constant throughout history.

It was the breakdown of the centralized Han government in A.D. 220 that created the conditions conducive for Buddhism to gain a stronger entree. On the one hand, the Han period ended with a large amount of social unrest. On the other, from the 3rd to the 6th century A.D., China lacked a single, strong centralized government, and the entire region that had belonged to the Han empire broke into multiple competing states. In the north the conditions were further exacerbated by the domination of several "non-Chinese" groups. These alleged barbarians embraced and patronized Buddhism fervently. Some suggest that Buddhist monks were welcome as sort of court magicians who, through their prayers and spells, assured the rulers of prosperity and military victories. Buddhism, perhaps simply because it was non-Chinese, might have also represented a means of preserving some kind of ethnic identity in the midst of the pressure to sinicize. Whatever the reason, the adoption of Buddhism by non-Chinese rulers in the north provided it with strong channels of entry into Chinese society in general.

The Formation and Development of Chinese Buddhist Thought

One of the most immediate problems facing the foreign monks who brought Buddhism to China was how to convey highly metaphysical and abstract concepts into a culture that lacked these notions and to translate them into a language that lacked the vocabulary to do so. The immediate solution was to employ terms and concepts from both Confucianism and Taoism, an indigenous philosophy that was more mystical than Confucianism, as vehicles for expression and translation. For example, the Taoist term *wuwei,* meaning non-action, was used to translate the Buddhist concept of Nirvana, and certain Confucian virtues were paired with Buddhist precepts. But, from the very beginning, Taoism and Buddhism were the most closely linked. Although their relationship would undergo differing phases of closeness and separateness, Buddhism and Taoism continued to interact with and influence each other throughout the course of history.

Perhaps as a device to make Buddhism more palatable to the Chinese, a Han period text already refers to the apochryphal story of Laozi (a major Taoist figure) departing for the west and turning up in India as the historical Buddha. (This legend was later used against Buddhists by Taoists who claimed that Buddhism was merely a corrupt form of Taoism.) In addition, during this initial period of Buddhist development, other subtle changes crept into Chinese Buddhism. For example, the position of women, relatively strong in Indian Buddhism, weakened considerably in Chinese Buddhism. It was through the efforts of the 5th century Central Asian Buddhist monk and translator Kumarajiva, who knew both Sanskrit and Chinese, that Buddhism finally developed its own vocabulary and achieved an intellectual position distinct from Taoism.

The various forms of Chinese Buddhism essentially belong to the Mahayana school. The earliest translated texts from Kumarajiva's workshop confirm this preference. For example, he translated the *Lotus Sutra,* a fundamental Mahayana text that became the doctrine of the later Tiantai sect and that inspired much Chinese Buddhist sculpture and painting. According to this text, this doctrine was presented before a huge assembly of bodhisattvas, arhats, monks and minor divinities, including *nagas* (water serpent spirits) and demons. The Buddha announced he would preach and that the doctrine would be difficult to understand. Five thousand offended doubters left. A stupa of dazzling colors then appeared in the sky together with music and perfume. The stupa contained the relics of the extinct Buddha, *Phrabutaratna,* who had vowed to materialize when the *Lotus Sutra* was preached. Sakyamuni (the historical Buddha) rose in the air, opened the stupa with a touch of his finger and joined Phrabutaratna on the throne. This heavenly stupa is shown on the front, and the two seated Buddhas on the lower register of the back of the stela dated A.D. 575 in The University Museum Rotunda (see page 22). As is fitting with Mahayana doctrine, the Buddha was no longer a mere enlightened human being, he was divine, a god. The power of the bodhisattvas to help all mankind was declared.

Another important Mahayana text, also translated by Kumarajiva, is the *Vimalakirti Nirdesa Sutra,* a document which stresses the importance of the layman as opposed to the ascetic dwelling in the monastery. According to the text, Vimalakirti, a famous philosopher and Buddhist layman, fell ill. When Sakyamuni asked his disciples to visit Vimalakirti, they refused for they had all been bested in previous discussions with him and felt unworthy. Finally Manjusri, the bodhisattva of wisdom, agreed to call on the philosopher. After engaging in a lively philosophical debate, Manjusri finally asked what was the essence of Buddhism. The philosopher answered with complete silence which was praised by Manjusri as the "thundering silence" of Vimalakirti. This sutra was good Buddhist propaganda among the Chinese intellectual elite since Vimalakirti was not only a Buddhist but a Confucian gentleman and scholar as well. Vimalakirti had also attained great wisdom and insight without the rejection of earthly

Set of five marble images representing the Buddha flanked by two bodhisattvas and two monks. Northern Qi, China; 6th century A.D. Buddha: H. 52.07 cm. Bodhisattvas: H. 43.18 cm. Monks: H. 40.64 cm.

ties such as celibacy. The debate between Manjusri and Vimalakirti is represented in the middle register on the back of the same stela dated A.D. 575 in the Rotunda of The University Museum (see page 22).

It was during this Six Dynasties period (A.D. 220–581) that Buddhism enjoyed its first real flush of popularity and firmly embedded itself in Chinese soil. The earliest extant Buddhist art in China dates from this period. Yet, whatever art China took from India had somehow to be made to fit within a Chinese context. For example, the Chinese did not adopt the most typical Indian Buddhist monument, the solid hemispherical stupa. The pagoda, the Chinese equivalent, was quite probably inspired by descriptions of the tower built by the Kushan king Kanishka (see Introduction, above), a wooden building of 13 stories with a spire threaded by 13 golden disks. (The Chinese faithfully kept the uneven number of stories, and the umbrella disks.) The pagoda was a type of structure not uncomfortably alien to them because they could relate it to the royal and memorial towers of their own landscape. On the other hand, they did take to the cave temples in the manner of the Indian rockcut establishments. The earliest Chinese example is found at Yungang, where at least 20 large and about the same number of small shrines were cut into soft sandstone in the early 5th century. These were constructed by the non-Chinese rulers of the Wei (A.D. 386–535).

When the Wei rulers moved their court to Luoyang in A.D. 498, they began to construct the cave temples at Longmen, about 10 miles from the capital. The dark hard limestone was a better medium for carving than the coarse sandstone of Yungang. An example of Longmen sculpture is the small relief of a seated bodhisattva at the entrance to the Rotunda. A beautiful example of the same Wei style with its elongated and linear rhythms is the Museum's gilt bronze Maitreya dated A.D. 536 (see page 54).

The Flourishing of Chinese Buddhism

In addition to this initial patronage by "barbarian" rulers, Buddhism was also adopted by both the Chinese elite, concentrated in the Yangtze region, and by the peasantry during this period. Thus, during the Chinese reunification of China, first under the short-lived Sui Dynasty (581–618) and then under the more enduring Tang Dynasty (618–907), Buddhism continued to receive imperial patronage and further served as a unifying mechanism. The Tang capital, Changan (today's Xi'an), and the surrounding countryside were filled with monks, nuns and monasteries, many of the latter serving as models for the temples and monasteries in Japan. It is no wonder that the Tang period is frequently referred to as the "golden age" of Chinese Buddhism.

The Tang period, a time of internationalism for

China, tolerated many religions. The second Tang emperor, Taizong (r. 627–649), for example, was personally a Taoist, but supported Confucianism and respected Buddhism so much that he personally went to meet the Buddhist monk Xuanzang (see below) on his return from India loaded with Buddhist sutras.

The Tang period also witnessed a new flurry of pilgrimages to northern India where Buddhist centers of learning flourished. Central Asia still functioned as an important transit area, although the increasing Islamizing of the region prompted greater use of the southern sea route. The famous monk and translator Xuanzang traveled to India at this time (629–645) and brought back important new Mahayanist scriptures. His travels were later fictionalized in the highly popular Chinese novel known in English as *Monkey* or *Journey to the West.*

The Tang period witnessed the emergence of new schools of Buddhism that were based on Indian counterparts, but that became uniquely Chinese. For example, there is the Jingtu or Pure Land school which was heavily devotional and in which salvation rested on total reliance and faith in Amitabha (Chinese: Amitofo), the Buddha of Infinite Light who presided over the Western Paradise (the Pure Land). This school became very popular in Japan, where it is known as Jodo. And there is the Tiantai school which focused its attention on the *Lotus Sutra.* Perhaps the most uniquely Chinese school to emerge during this period was the Meditation, or Chan, school (later known in Japan as Zen). This 7th century blend of mainly Taoist and Mahayanist elements held that the Universal Buddha-nature is present within all of us and that it is attainable through meditation and through direct communication between master and disciple without intermediary reliance on texts. Many of the Chinese schools from the Tang period reappear slightly later in Japan. In China itself, the Chan and Pure Land schools remained the dominant ones long after other schools had lost their distinction.

During the Tang period another unique characteristic of Chinese Buddhism appeared—the concept of Patriarchs. In imitation of Chinese society itself which is strongly patriarchal and patrilineal, Buddhist schools began to organize their masters and pupils into neat genealogies, tracing the spiritual masters of each school back to a real or imaginary founder.

The Tang period was also a time of a great flowering of the arts, particularly sculpture. The influence of the Gupta Indian style (the Gupta empire ruled from A.D. 320–535; the sculpture is characterized by restrained sensuousness, with smooth, soft surfaces, and facial expressions exhibiting a certain sweetness) softened the austere Wei and Sui period images, and added a sensuousness that obviously appealed to the more sophisticated Tang public (see the pair of stone bodhisattvas in the Rotunda).

Standing gilt bronze Guanyin. China, 11th c. A.D. H. 71.12 cm., W. 25.4 cm.

The Sangha or monastic community was particularly strong and prosperous during this time, a condition that was eventually to work against Buddhism when the central state decided once again to assert greater control over the Buddhist community. The growing strength and wealth of the Buddhist temple complexes worried not a few members of the ruling elite. Thus, the late Tang period witnessed a resurgence of Confucian attitudes. The resulting suppression of Buddhism in 842–845 involved the defrocking of monks and nuns and the disbanding of many of the large monasteries. The attack, however, focused on the professional clergy and not the practicing laity.

Later Developments in Chinese Buddhism

In post-Tang period China, Buddhism did not disappear as many scholars have suggested; its focus merely shifted. Buddhism no longer attracted the finest minds. The majority of China's intellectual energy was directed toward the bureaucratic examinations and the essays and the poetry of the Confucian literati. It is important to note, however, that Song period (960–1279) Neo-Confucian thought owes much of its inspiration to Buddhism.

Small shrine containing blue-skinned image that sits outside one of the main halls in the Nan Shan Si Monastery, Wu Tai Shan, Shanxi, China. Photograph by H. Peters.

Despite this re-emergence of the ideal of the Confucian bureaucratic scholar-official, Buddhism continued to play a strong role on the local, popular level. The village priest had always been a less educated, perhaps even self-taught individual, whose rituals and practices drew not only from Buddhism but from popular Taoism and popular Confucianism as well. This trend simply continued in post-Tang period China, resulting in a popular religion that incorporated elements from all three. Taoist gods, local earth gods and ancestors, and the Buddha and various bodhisattvas could all be found in a single temple. Furthermore, the attending ritual specialist could be either a Buddhist monk, or a Taoist priest.

In addition, many gods and goddesses changed shape and personality, the effect of merging gods from one religion with another. For example, the male bodhisattva Guanyin (Sanskrit: Avalokitesvara), recognized for his extreme compassion and mercy, gradually merged with a local goddess also known for her compassion and who was further associated with fertility. Guanyin, thus, in later times frequently appears in the female form.

Temples offered a melange of popular beliefs and are consequently a nightmare for the student of art history and religion. Sorting out the different elements became more and more difficult with the passing of centuries. Buddhist priests on this level played and continue to play an important role in the life events of their villages. They officiate at funerals and weddings, tend to certain ancestral rites and perform exorcisms, and pray for rain using the efficacy of their chants and spells. In a sense, the initial attraction of Buddhism, its spells and magic, in the end lingers on.

On the upper levels of society, however, Buddhism was not completely discarded. An interesting development is the role Lamaism or Tibetan Buddhism plays in later Chinese history (see section on Tibet for a fuller discussion of Lamaism). For political reasons, Lamaism continued to receive patronage on an imperial level during the Yuan (1271–1368), Ming (1368–1644) and Qing (1644–1911) periods—and especially during the first and last. Consequently many Buddhist temples extant today exhibit a unique blend of Pure Land and Lamaist elements. A classic triad of Sakyamuni, Amitabha and Maitreya may sit on the principal altar in the main hall, but tankas (Tibetan Buddhist religious paintings—see section on Tibet) may be found hanging on the sides, multi-armed esoteric images of bodhisattvas serve as focal points for the secondary halls, and sometimes a horrifying blue-faced image draped in a garland of skulls occupies a small shrine attached to the corner of a building.

Is China a Buddhist country, or was it ever? China was never and isn't a Buddhist country in the same sense Southeast Asian countries like Thailand or Burma are, nor is it Buddhist like Japan. In China, Buddhism

Artisans creating new Buddhist images for Xian Tong Si Temple in Wu Tai Shan, Shanxi, China. Photograph by H. Peters.

always remained somewhat suspect to the ruling elite—it was, in the end, a foreign religion.

The Position of Buddhism in Post-Liberation China

Buddhism fell on hard times after the 1949 revolution. Although Buddhist monks and nuns were not initially persecuted, their land, which represented their principal means of support, was seized by the new communist government. The Cultural Revolution (c. 1966–78) wreaked considerably more havoc, as troops of young red guards roamed the cities and countryside with license to smash all relics of China's "evil, feudal past." Consequently, the images and interiors of many temples and monasteries were destroyed or severely damaged during this time. Since 1980, with China's return to normalcy, the government has permitted, and even encouraged, the restoration of its cultural heritage, Buddhism included (see above).

What seemed at first to be merely a restoration of the monasteries and temples as empty museums has passed into a phase of the actual revival of Buddhism itself. The older monks have returned to their temples and resumed their prayers and rituals. Oddly enough, young men and some women have also joined monasteries and nunneries. They have voluntarily decided to undergo the training to become monks or nuns.

The seriousness of their motivation and dedication is still untested. For some, the decision to join a monastery appears to represent a kind of rebellious whim, much to the dismay of their socialist, atheistic parents. But their endurance can be short-lived since the romance of meditative monkhood is quickly shattered by the reality of the harsh conditions coupled with the severe discipline within the monastery. One poor father on his way to pick up his son from a monastery in Wu Tai Shan (one of China's sacred mountains, located in

Daily afternoon Buddhist chanting at the Jade Buddhist Temple, Shanghai, China. Photograph by H. Peters.

Shansi Province) sounded much like contemporary fathers anywhere when he described his situation. "My son wanted to become a monk—and who can stop young people these days? But then when he got to the monastery the food was bad, he wasn't permitted to sleep, the head monk beat him, and now he wants to come home!" For others, their intentions may be serious and their decision to join a monastery could lead to a lifetime commitment.

The Buddhist temples are crowded. Bustling crowds jostle you everywhere on the temple grounds. But the majority of people seem to be on a holiday and they treat the whole experience with great amusement, intently staring at the monks and nuns as though they were performers in some bizarre form of drama. Yet, the donation boxes are packed with cash—some in rather large denominations. Rumor has it that the monasteries are doing very well these days. The least likely persons can be observed kowtowing with requests to one of the Buddhas.

China will not become a major Buddhist center in Asia, but this resurgence of Buddhist fervor, especially among the rural people, emphasizes the eclectic and practical nature of the Chinese people and society. Now, as in the past, the Chinese people are willing to try a little of something foreign and different, and if it works, it is neatly tucked into their continually growing and changing corpus of beliefs and traditions.

HP & EL

THE INTRODUCTION OF BUDDHISM TO JAPAN

Traditional Japanese historical sources date the introduction of Buddhism to Japan to A.D. 552 when the Korean Emperor Kimmei presented Buddhist sutras and a Buddhist image to the ruler of Japan as a gift. The initial skepticism about the new religion gave way as the magical and protective powers associated with Buddhism began to prove themselves more effective than those of Shinto. The Empress Suiko (r. 592–628) not only proclaimed state patronage of Buddhism, but she herself personally embraced Buddhism and withdrew from court life into a nunnery. Her nephew, Prince Shotoku, who served as regent from 575–621, strongly supported Buddhism. He is considered the founder of Japanese Buddhism and sculptures of him, often as a child, were sometimes placed in Buddhist temples as objects of worship (see page 11).

Korea has an important Buddhist tradition and served as the initial area of transmission of this religion from China to Japan. Unfortunately, because the Museum's collection lacks Korean material, we have had to omit a Korean section.

The Relationship of Buddhism and Shintoism

Shinto, or "Way of the Gods," is the name attached to the pre-Buddhist religion in Japan. Shinto expressed a reverence for nature and an intimacy with the sacred. Originally it lacked a scriptual corpus and an organized priesthood. At the time of the introduction of Buddhism into Japan, Shinto was still a simple religion concerned with fertility and pollution. The gods, or *kami,* did not have anthropomorphic forms. They were animistic and were associated with specific locations identified as holy. Sometimes the presence of kami was marked by a small shrine and a sacred object such as a bronze mirror or sword. There is no evidence that the name "Shinto" existed in the pre-Buddhist period. The systematic organization of Shinto and the anthropomorphization of the kami are direct responses to the influence of and competition with Buddhism.

As early as the 8th century A.D., Gyogi, a Buddhist monk of the Hosso sect, fused Shinto and Buddhism. He considered them two forms of the same truth, and in 747 he carried a Buddhist relic to the shrine of the Sun Goddess (the most important kami goddess) at Ise and asked her about the Buddha. Her response was favorable, and thereafter the Shinto gods were thought of as local manifestations of Buddhist divinities. This event marks the movement that syncretized the two religions into what is called "Dual Shinto."

The Major Schools of Japanese Buddhism

Although some of the earliest Buddhist schools during the Nara period (A.D. 645–784) were considered Mahayanist, in fact, they were Theravadan in practice. They concentrated on an elite clergy who sought individual salvation. The religion's only popular appeal was in its use of ritual and magic.

The appearance of Esoteric Buddhism in the early Heian period (9th century) marked an important shift in this trend. Esoteric Buddhism forms part of the Tantric Buddhist tradition, which developed in India probably around the 5th century A.D. It evolved a pantheon heavily influenced by Hinduism and exhibited a pronounced interest in magic and female deities. The term Tantric comes from a group of texts called the *tantras* (texts added to Mahayana canon in India during the 5th century A.D.), which describe spells, formulas, iconography and rites. They are manuals that emphasize the practical effects of magic. Tantricism can furthermore be divided into two schools: left-handed and right-handed. Left-handed Tantricism (Vajrayana or Thunderbolt) emphasizes the feminine counterparts (saktis) of the deities and includes ritual sexual intercourse. This is the form of Tantricism found in Nepal and Tibet. Right-handed Tantricism emphasizes the masculine deities and does not emphasize sexual elements. This is the branch of Tantricism that spread to China and Japan.

Two schools of Esoteric Buddhism developed in Japan during the 9th century, Tendai (Chinese: Tiantai) and Shingon. Both were founded by Japanese monks who studied in China. Tendai, founded by the monk Saicho, combined a mixture of Zen (Chinese: Chan) meditation practice, a focus on the *Lotus Sutra* text and some esoteric teaching.

Kukai, founder of the Shingon sect (Shingon means the "true word," which is passed down from teacher to pupil), went to China in 804 and returned to Japan as the 8th Patriarch of the esoteric tradition.

Kukai used magical charms, special incantations (*mantras*) and ritual gestures (*mudras*) as part of the spectacular and mysterious rituals that formed an integral part of Esoteric Buddhism. The impressive rituals with the elaborate costumes of the priests appealed to a much broader audience. Kukai's own personal charisma fostered many legends.

A brief explanation of the core of Shingon belief is essential because it assumes a dominant role in the iconography of Shingon art. Shingon envisions a pantheism in which the whole universe is seen as a manifestation of the Cosmic Buddha Vairochana (Japanese: Dainichi Nyorai). Even other Buddhas are regarded as manifestations of Vairochana.

Art played a significant role in Shingon Buddhism since it was believed that art could effectively convey the profound meaning of the sutras. Art included not just painting and sculpture, but music and ritual as well. In Shingon art, the sacred manifestations are more than merely aesthetically pleasing; they embody the profound, mysterious forces that compose the divinity. *Mandalas,* or cosmic, sacred diagrams, are important to Shingon. The mandalas are sometimes formed around a group of five Buddhas known in Japanese as: Dainichi, Amida, Shaka, Miroku and Yakushi. Dainichi is the central Cosmic Buddha from which all others emanate. Amida is the Buddha of Infinite Light—Lord of the Western Paradise. Shaka is the historical Buddha, the man who achieved profound enlightenment. Miroku represents the Buddha who is yet to come, and Yakushi, Lord of the Eastern Paradise, is associated with disease and curing. The five Buddhas are commonly referred to as the Five Dhyani (meditation) Buddhas and occur both in Shingon art and in Tibetan art.

Bodhisattvas were also frequently depicted. Kannon (Skt.: Avalokitesvara) is the bodhisattva of compassion and mercy. Monju (Skt.: Manjusri), bodhisattva of wisdom, always rides his lion; he carries the sword of wisdom in his right hand and a scroll symbolizing spiritual knowledge in his left. Fugen (Skt.: Samantabhadra), with whom he is frequently paired, embodies goodness and rides a white elephant (see page 10). They sometimes form a triad with Sakyamuni, the historical Buddha.

Another important category in Shingon art is the Myo-o or "Knowledge Kings." These are a fierce class of protective divinities. The Myo-o usually appear in groups of five. Their number five coordinates with the four cardinal points, and the center. Fudo Myo-o, the "Unmoveable" (possibly a transformation of the Hindu god Shiva), is the most commonly depicted of the Myo-o. He stands at the center of the group. Fudo's plump black-skinned body with his ferocious expression, bulging eyes and fangs presents an awesome sight to believers and unbelievers alike. Fudo carries a lasso in his right hand to save sufferers and a *vajra*-hilted sword

Painted Kakemono (hanging scroll) depicting Sakyamuni on a lotus. Japan, 18th to 19th century. L. 134 cm., W. 40.5 cm.

Mokugyo. "Fish" drum that is beaten to accompany the chanting of sutras. Japan, 19th century. Lacquered wood with red and black paint. H. 78.58 cm., W. 92.28 cm.

in his left to cut down evil (see page 12). He is frequently depicted together with two of his eight attendants, Kongara and Seitaka.

The inconography of these esoteric images is very precise. Rules concerning the form and significance of the sculpture and paintings appear in the Buddhist scriptures themselves and in iconographic model books.

Although Shingon Buddhism remains an important sect in Japan to the present day, the most popular and widespread school was and is Jodo (Pure Land) which focuses on Amida, the Buddha of Infinite Light who rules the Western Paradise. This school appeared as early as the 10th century, but its popularity peaked during the late 11th and early 12th centuries. The school had popular appeal because of its simplified philosophy with a strong emphasis on pure and true faith in the salvation of the Amida. Simple recitation of the devotional formula, "Namu Amida Butsu" (Hail Amida Buddha), became sufficient to assure rebirth in the Western Paradise. The multiple repetitions of the "Nembutsu" became important, and one 11th century noble notes in his diary having repeated the formula as many as 170,00 times in one day!

The belief in the saving capacity of Amida Buddha was manifested in a very distinctive art form—the *raigo* paintings and sculpture. As a person neared death, he was handed a cord attached to a painting or sculpture of Amida Buddha who was "coming" (*rai* means "to come" in Japanese) to "greet" (*go* in Japanese) the deceased and guide him to his Western Paradise. This very graphic and physical interpretation of the belief in salvation via the Amida Buddha reflects the character of Pure Land Buddhism.

The late 12th and early 13th centuries mark the appearance of the Zen school of Buddhism in Japan. The term Zen (Chinese: Chan) means "meditation" and is derived from the Indian word *dhyana*. Some form of meditation is found in most Buddhist schools, but Chan began as a separate school in 7th century China. The school focused on meditation as the primary means to deliverance and enlightenment based on one's own efforts.

The long hours of required meditation in Zen temples and monasteries were punctuated by chanting, accompanied by a wooden drum called *mokugyo* ("wooden fish"; see left). The Zen tradition embodied esoteric aspects in its reliance on direct transmission from master to disciple. This custom resulted in complex genealogies of important Zen masters or Patriarchs that reflected the line of transmission of the Dharma (Buddhist truth). A school of portraiture developed in Zen art in which highly respected Patriarchs were preserved in painting or sculpture. Our seated figure of a Patriarch (see page 13) possibly depicts Bodhidharma, the so-called first Patriarch of Zen who transmitted the doctrine from India to China.

Zen played an important role in the development of Japanese aesthetics. Eisai and Dogen, the two early founders of Zen in Japan, were strongly attracted to Chinese culture and brought over Chinese potters, carpenters and artists. To this day, Zen influence is strongly felt in Japanese architecture, gardening, ceramics, painting and literature.

The final major development in Japanese Buddhism came with Nichiren (1222–1282). The distinctiveness of Nichiren's Buddhism lay in his vision of Japan as the country from which his doctrine would spread throughout the world. Nichiren Buddhism became highly fused with a nationalistic character and missionary fervor hitherto unheard of in Buddhism. The sect gave rise to such a degree of intolerance that it was initially banned, and Nichiren was imprisoned. Today, Nichirenism and its offshoots remain influential in Japan.

Buddhism's Later Development in Japan

During the Tokugawa period (A.D. 1615–1867), the government strictly controlled Buddhism, and the religion tended to stagnate. Part of this control required that every citizen register at his or her local Buddhist temple for census purposes, and thus temples became strongly associated with generations of families.

The Meiji period (A.D. 1868–1912) witnessed a brief but devastating persecution of Buddhism coupled with the elevation of Shinto to the level of a state cult and religion. By the late 19th century both Buddhism and Shinto were forced to compete with strong Western influences. Post-World War II Buddhism is a multifaceted institution, with a strong hold on the lives of some Japanese and almost no hold on the lives of others. The many new sects that have sprung up in Japan since World War II are not strictly Buddhist, reflecting a combination of Buddhism, Shintoism, Christianity and even Shamanism. We can view Buddhist development in Japan on two levels. On the one hand, there is the more scholarly Buddhism which developed in the temple complexes and monasteries. This aspect of Buddhism began as early as the 8th century and has continued to the present. Japan today is considered a major center for Buddhist learning and study. These centers, however, are distinct from Buddhist practice and worship on the popular level. The average Japanese villager or city dweller can be both a Shinto and a Buddhist. The two religions neither clash nor contradict each other. Both have their specific domain of worship, and the yearly calendar follows a cycle of intertwining Shinto and Buddhist festivals.

A principal focus in Buddhism is on funerary services. Prior to the introduction of Buddhism, the Japanese concept of an afterlife was little developed, though attention was paid to the spirits of the dead. Buddhism arrived with its built-in structure of hells, heavens and elaborate rituals performed to propitiate and aid the post-mortem spirits of one's deceased ancestors. Shinto, on the other hand, is more commonly associated with marriage and childbirth.

Traditionally, every home has its Buddhist area or space. Usually it takes the form of a *butsudan,* a large black lacquer cabinet, gilded with gold and ornamented with brass (see page 15). The expense and elegance of the butsudan, or household shrine, is determined by the wealth of the family. The butsudan serves as a repository for the family's ancestor tablets. It also houses a small statue of a Buddha or a bodhisattva, or a Buddhist scroll, which serves as the focus of daily worship. Other features include small bowls for water, rice and other food offerings, a vase for flowers, candles, metal and wooden bells, rosaries, incense and

Small portable shrine containing a small stupa reliquary. Japan, 19th century. Wood lacquered black, decorated with brass; gilded interior. H. 21.59 cm., W. 11.43 cm.

prayer books. Sometimes the cabinet held more secular items such as books, magazines or other small objects. Smaller, portable shrines were carried and used for worship by pilgrims and travelers (see pages 16 & 31).

In addition, most households also have a *kamidana,* a Shinto spiritshelf, located above the doorway in a corner of the anteroom or overhead in the entry, to assist in protecting the household against intrusion of harmful influences. The shelf contains an incense bowl and a small bowl for rice offerings and a tiny vase to hold a sprig of the *sakai* bush.

Although most people nominally belong to a Buddhist sect, it is not compulsory to attend temple meetings. Instead, the temple priests frequently go to the homes of their parishioners on important occasions to assist them in appropriate ceremonies.

By far the most widely observed festival in the Buddhist calendar is *bon,* held on the 13th–15th days of the 7th lunar month. The purpose of *bon* is to venerate the immediate ancestors. The house is cleaned, the family graves are tidied, and the ancestral tablets are brought out of their butsudan. The ancestors are invited back on this day to partake in a special feast of rice cakes, *mochi* (sticky rice) and fresh vegetables. Offerings may also be placed at the site of the family grave itself. In addition, many people set up special offerings for the "hungry ghosts," spirits who may not have any living descendants to care for them.

Although the ceremony is Buddhist, its completion reflects the close exchange of Buddhist and non-Buddhist beliefs. The departure of the ancestors is dramatically enacted by each family constructing a small straw boat into which they place some offerings and a lighted candle. Traditionally these boats were floated down the canals at midnight; however, most villages now burn their boats in a spectacular bonfire, much to the delight of the village children who stay awake specially for this event. Like many other popular festivals, bon combines elements from orthodox Buddhism and the folk traditions of India, China and Japan.

HP

Map showing main sites related to Buddhism mentioned in this handbook.

MANCHURIA
MONGOLIA
Sea of Japan
JAPAN
Kyoto
Nara
KOREA
ANG
Turfan
Yungang
WU TAI SHAN
Beijing
Yellow Sea
Changan (Xi'an)
Luoyang
Longmen
CHINA
East China Sea
TIBET
Pacific Ocean
Lhasa
Samye
BHUTAN
Bihar
Canton
BANGLA-DESH
BURMA
VIETNAM
LAOS
Luang Prabang
Gulf of Tonkin
South China Sea
PHILIPPINES
Pagan
Irrawady R.
Chiangmai
Vientiene
Pegu
Sukhothai
Mekong R.
Rangoon
Thaton
THAILAND
Champassak
Bay of Bengal
Chansen
Lopburi
Ayutthaya
CHAMPA
Angkor
Bangkok
CAMBODIA
Phnom Penh
Ho Chi Minh City (Saigon)
Oc-eo
Gulf of Siam
MALAYSIA
BORNEO
SUMATRA
750 1000 km
INDONESIA
Jakarta
DIENG PLATEAU
JAVA
Borobudur

MAJOR BUDDHIST EVENTS

600 BC

Life of the historical Buddha (ca. 560–480)
First Buddhist Council (ca. 480)

400 BC

Second Buddhist Council (ca. 380)
Third Buddhist Council (ca. 250)
Buddhism introduced into Sri Lanka (247)
King Ashoka patronizes Buddhism (269–232)

200 BC

Mahayana beliefs begin to develop (2nd c. B.C.–3rd c. A.D.)
Fourth Buddhist Council (ca. 100)
Theravada Buddhist scriptures first written down in Sri Lanka in Pali script (89–77)

0

Earliest images of the Buddha (1st c.)
Buddhism spreads to China via Central Asia (1st c.)
Earliest appearance of Buddhist object found in Thailand (1st c.)

200

Buddhist mission reaches Vietnam from China (ca. 220)
Buddhism becomes widespread in China (3rd–6th c.)
Hinduism begins to replace Buddhism in India (4th–6th c.)

400

Monk Faxian's pilgrimage from China to India and Southeast Asia (399–414)
First Buddhist missions to Burma, Sumatra and Java (5th c.)
Buddhist persecution in China (445–446)
Buddhism begins to penetrate Cambodia (4th–6th c.)
Buddhism introduced to Japan via Korea (552)

600

Buddhism declared a state religion in Japan (594)
Monk Xuanzang's pilgrimage from China to India (629–45)
I Jing's pilgrimage from China to India and Southeast Asia (671–693)
Construction of Borobudur (750–780)

800

Buddhism spreads to Tibet (7th–8th c.)
Japanese monks Saicho and Kukai return from China (805 & 806)
Buddhist persecution in China (843–845)

1000

Construction of Angkor Wat begins (1113–1150)

1200

Theravada Buddhism becomes a state religion in Thailand (1360)

1400

Emergence of dGe-lugs-pa (Yellow Hat) sect in Tibet, together with institution of Dalai Lama (15th c.)

1600

1800

Shinto resurgence, Buddhism denounced in Japan (1868–71)

1900

State Shinto dissolved in Japan, Buddhism revived (1945)
Buddhism persecuted in China (1949–1978), now revived
2500th anniversary of Buddha's Enlightenment (1956)

BUDDHISM IN TIBET

Tibet, Land of the Snows, is not the completely bleak, mountainous region people imagine. Intersected by broad and fertile valleys, southern Tibet supports a large sedentary, agricultural population which feeds the region. Although relatively isolated by its climate and terrain, Tibet was nonetheless linked with its neighbors through ethnic, cultural and religious ties. Tibet's towns and cities have also functioned as important trade centers, thereby linking them both with India to the south and China to the east.

Tibet's status as an independent country has varied considerably during the last 1500 years. In the past, Tibet's boundaries included the modern Himalayan kingdoms of Ladakh, Kashmir and Sikkim, as well as portions of the modern Chinese provinces of Qinghai and Sichuan. The current political boundaries of Tibet, now an autonomous region of China, do not reflect the entire distribution of Tibetan people and culture.

Tibet is renowned for its special brand of Buddhism known as Lamaism. The term lama means "superior one" in Tibetan and is applied generally to all Buddhist monks. Although Tibetan Buddhism is frequently referred to as Tantric Buddhism (a sect influenced by Hinduism and concerned with magic, see above), in reality Lamaism is an amalgam of early, native shamanist beliefs combined with a cult of divine kingship, and imported Buddhist concepts which reflect both Mahayanist and Tantric influences. The Tantric influences do play an important role and receive a high degree of visibility because of the distinctive Tibetan art style and iconography. Tibetan Buddhism also evolved a unique liturgical and analytic tradition which, along with its art tradition, reflects Indian, Chinese and indigenous influences. Lamaism is also distinguished by the unique role monks or lamas play in Tibetan society, illustrated best in the person of the Dalai Lama.

The Introduction and History of Buddhism in Tibet

Buddhism appears in Tibet sometime during the 7th to 8th centuries A.D. According to tradition, Buddhism was introduced during the reign of King Srong-btsan (d. A.D. 650), first unifier of Tibet. Contemporary documents and inscriptions, however, do not confirm this tradition. On the contrary, they clearly identify King Srong-btsan as a strong supporter of the 7th century indigenous religion which regarded the king as divine. The king's divinity was further linked with the mountains, the home of the fierce indigenous gods. Thus, although Buddhism may have been present in Tibet by the 7th century A.D., it was not yet as widely accepted as scholars formerly believed.

By the 8th century, however, Buddhism's presence was more marked, and by 792 some important features of Tibetan Buddhism had already appeared. First, from the beginning the religion enjoyed royal patronage, with lamas holding important positions in the political hierarchy. Second, the local Tibetan deities had been incorporated into the Buddhist pantheon as protectors of the faith. And, third, the precedence of Indian Buddhism over Chinese was determined, with special preference given to Tantric practices.

Despite Buddhism's 8th century beginnings in Tibet, it is the 11th century that marks the significant period of Buddhist development in Tibet. At that time, the Indian monk Atisa (982–1054) arrived, bringing in the cult of Avalokitesvara (Chinese: Guanyin), the bodhisattva of compassion and mercy. Atisa reinforced Tantric practices and stressed certain meditative procedures and yogic powers. Among the several sects that were established during this period, the Sa-skya-pa (Saskya) dominated. The Saskya and other schools dating from this period are sometimes referred to as the Red Hats because of the reddish color of the monks' costumes.

Much enamored with the Saskyas, the Mongols converted to Lamaism in the 13th century and appointed the head lama of the Saskyas as regent of Tibet. This move established a precedent that dominated Tibetan politics until the Chinese takeover in 1951. In addition, the belief in succession by reincarnation also appeared, and thereafter, the successor to a deceased head lama was sought in a child born after the death of the lama.

Finally, the 15th century witnessed the emergence of the dGe-lugs-pa school, popularly referred to as the Yellow Hats because of the color of the headgear. The founder, Tsong-kha-pa, established two temples in the vicinity of Lhasa, and one of these, Drepung, became the largest monastery in the whole of Tibet, housing at its peak nearly 1500 monks.

The institution of naming the head lama the Dalai Lama, which in Tibetan means the "Ocean (of Wisdom) Lama," began with the Yellow Hats. It was the fifth Dalai Lama, Ngag-dbang-blo-bzang-rgya-mtsho (1617–1682), who won victory over both the secular ruler and the heads of other Buddhist schools and established himself as the undisputed leader of Tibet. The fifth Dalai Lama also established other important markers of his power and prestige. He regarded himself as not only the reincarnation of his predecessor, but also of the bodhisattva Avalokitesvara. He built the magnificant Potala—symbol of his immense power, whose name comes from the sacred mountain in south India which is regarded as the seat of Avalokitesvara.

Although Ngag-dbang-blo-bzang-rgya-mtsho did not eradicate the remaining other Buddhist schools, the Yellow Hats with their Dalai Lama were now and continued to be the dominant force, both religious and secular, until 1951. In that year, Chinese troops marched outright into Tibet, taking full control. The eastern portions of Tibet were absorbed into other existing Chinese provinces, and the remaining core, redefined as the Tibet Autonomous Region, was subject to direct Chinese control. In 1959 the 14th Dalai Lama fled to India where he resides today. During the more than 30 years that followed, Tibet was subjected periodically to full-scale attack and persecution of the core of its cultural traditions, especially Buddhism. During the Cultural Revolution, which rocked the foundations of China during the late 1960s and 70s, Tibetan temples and art were systematically destroyed.

Painted wooden dancer's mask worn in ritual plays and dances performed in monasteries. Probably from Nepal, 19th to 20th century. H. 48.26 cm., W. 25.4 cm.

China's current policy of economic incentive coupled with an unprecedented relaxation of control over individuals' lives has permitted the Tibetan people to restore and reopen some of their temples and monasteries. A small group of Buddhist monks have returned to the temples; however, it is not easy to replace or restore the vast amount of material that was either lost or destroyed. Collections in museums like ours have become important preservers of this tradition.

Tibetan Ritual and Religious Life

Religion permeated every aspect of daily life in Tibet. Before 1959, there were approximately 3,000 monasteries in Tibet occupied by nearly 20% of the adult male population. The monks living in the monasteries were celibate and maintained the strict rules of the Sangha of the Buddhist community.

But in addition to the cloistered monk communities, self-styled religious adepts and a married clergy also existed. The married clergy were exempt from monastic vows, but kept either a bodhisattva vow to strive for the salvation of all sentient beings, or a Tantric vow to strive to attain collective salvation in one lifetime. They played respected roles in the community and worked together with monastic monks in officiating at household ceremonies involving birth, death and illness.

The lay population, in general, while extremely devout, left questions of a metaphysical or philosophical nature to the clergy. Their concern lay in carrying out the physical acts of devotion which established their faith and belief.

Temples and Monasteries

The temples and monasteries housed the communities of celibate lamas who tended to the spiritual maintenance of the world order. In addition to daily chants and rituals, the temples staged several large-scale ceremonies and festivals throughout the year, such as the New Year festival, a festival of cosmic renewal, and the harvest festival. These drew huge crowds from miles around who came to participate in and see the elaborate and colorful festivities. On these occasions, hundreds of monks performed sacred dances and plays in the open courtyards wearing elaborate masks (see left) and costumes. Huge banners were unfurled down hillsides (see page 37), and giant paintings and images could be viewed. During these times, the temples served as important centers for focusing religious energy and devotion.

An enormous appliqued banner displayed once a year on Monlam Chemo ("Great Prayer Festival") in February, Labrang, Amdo, Tibet. Photographed by Griebenow, ca. 1922–40. Collection of the Newark Museum.

Ritual Implements

Certain items are found in both temples and on domestic altars but were used specifically by the priests. For example, the bell and the *vajra* (Tibetan: *dorje,* a sceptre with four pronged ends) are two very important and frequently used ritual implements. The vajra, also called the "Thunderbolt," is the attribute of Vajrapani, the special protector of Sakyamuni. The vajra, considered masculine, symbolizes indestructibility and compassion. It is always paired with the bell whose handle must match the vajra in size. The bell is feminine and symbolizes wisdom. The union of the two objects symbolizes the supreme truth. In Tantric ritual, the vajra is held in the right hand and the bell in the left and the two are manipulated by the priests (see right).

Other items, such as rosaries and prayer wheels, are used by both laymen and priests. Rosaries, which are found in India, China and Japan as well, are thought to have evolved from Hindu prayer beads. According to tradition, Tibetan rosaries have 108 beads.

Prayer wheels are especially diagnostic of Tibetan ritual objects. They were an ingenious device created to produce multiple prayers with a flick of the wrist. Rolls of written prayers or *mantras* (symbolic sounds which have the ability to invoke spiritual powers and harmony) were sealed inside the cylindrical top, and with each spin of the wheel, all the prayers and mantras were, in effect, repeated. The smaller wheels were carried by priests and devout laymen in their hands (see page 38), but large-scale versions were placed on roofs or in streams where they were turned incessantly by wind or water, or were placed by temple entrances and were turned by monks or pilgrims (see page 38).

Teapots, water ewers, small bowls and butter lamps are found on domestic or temple altars (see page 39). All these items played a role in the daily offerings and rituals. The butter lamps, symbolizing the sacred

Silver bell (ghanta) and brass vajra. These are two important ritual objects used by lamas. Bell: H. 19.07 cm., W. 10.16 cm. Vajra: L. 11.43. cm.

Women turning large prayer wheels, Labrang Monastery (founded 1709), Amdo, Tibet. Photographed by Griebenow, ca. 1922–40. Collection of the Newark Museum.

Two prayer wheels from Tibet, 19th to 20th century. L. *copper and wood, L. 21.59 cm.* R. *brass, wood and ivory, L. 26.67 cm.*

flame of Buddhism, were lit every evening. The small bowls contained offerings of water, tea and rice. They were refreshed daily, usually in the morning. The ewers and teapots were used for pouring the water and tea during the rituals.

Human skulls and bones were frequently used to make many Tibetan ritual items. For example, the skulls of holy men, which were particularly valued, became libation vessels which were lined with brass and encrusted with precious turquoise (see page 39). Where did this use of human bone come from? Skulls and bones are a sharp reminder of our own immortality and the transient nature of this world. Buddhist monks in India meditated on skulls for this very reason. But the excessive number of human skulls used both as ritual objects and musical instruments, and the depiction of skulls in ritual painting seem to reflect some deeper and perhaps pre-Buddhist shamanist aspect of Tibetan culture and society.

Other pre-Buddhist elements are clearly present in Tibetan Buddhism. Both in the temples and among the laymen we find the presence of ritual specialists who functioned as kinds of sorcerers or shamans. These specialists frequently employed the *phurpa,* a ritual dagger used to exorcise demons by literally stabbing the air and pinning down the demon inside a ritual space (see page 41). During exorcism rites, both the specialists and lamas sometimes wore elaborate aprons carved from human bone. The relationship between pre-Buddhist religious elements and Buddhist elements is indeed complex, but it is the combination of these elements that creates the uniqueness of Tibetan Buddhism.

Music and Ritual

Tibetan Buddhist monks developed a distinctive repertoire of sounds and movements which accompanied their rituals and meditation. They chanted and sang specific texts and mantras which invoked particular deities. Various kinds of drums, trumpets and cymbals, and mudras (ritual hand gestures) articulated and intensified the significance of the ritual. In addition, monks manipulated bells and vajras and incorporated other items, such as sets of symbol cards and the water ewers, into the slow, elaborate and deliberate ceremonial events. The figure on page 50 illustrates some of the instruments used during these ceremonies: the long telescopic brass trumpets which can expand to 16 feet, pairs of cymbals, skull drums and a trumpet made from a human thigh bone. Unlike the skulls used for the libation bowls, the trumpets were made from the thigh bones of criminals or men who had died a violent death. They apparently were more effective in scaring away demons and evil spirits.

Domestic Worship

The domestic altar found in every Tibetan's home, be it a house or a tent, is, in fact, a microcosm of the larger altars found in the temples and monasteries. Every alter would have at least one small icon or *tanka* (religious painting) which served as a focal point. Sometimes a grouping of three tankas might be placed in triptych fashion around an altar on top of which sat a central icon. It is important that the sacred image be placed higher than the other items found on the altar. This position indicates respect. In addition, every altar must have its assortment of butter lamps, small bowls, teapots and water ewers, described above, that were used not just for the daily offerings, but as part of special ceremonies which the household might commission.

Various ritual paraphernalia used by the priests

Objects found on a Tibetan Buddhist altar. 19th to 20th century. From l. *to* r.: *Temple teapot of copper trimmed with silver, H. 26.34 cm. Small wooden bowl lined with silver, H. 4.5 cm., D. 8 cm. Very small wooden bowl lined with silver, H. 2.3 cm. Water ewer of copper with brass cover and spout, H. 19 cm. Bronze(?) butter lamp, H. 6.7 cm.*

when they come to a family's home to perform certain ceremonies may be stored on the altar when not in use. In addition, prayer wheels and rosaries may be placed on the altar when not in use. Incense burners, another important ritual item, do not go on top of the altar, but either just in front of it, or on a lower shelf.

Finally, we find the ubiquitous Tibetan charm or relic box. No Tibetan ever left home without one, but when they were not in use, they too were usually kept on the domestic altar. The charm boxes were either worn strung around the neck (women) or slung around the chest (men; see page 40). They warded off evil spirits which Tibetans believed inhabited the earth, air and water. The contents of these boxes range from written prayers and small esoteric images to auspicious relics such as the robe fragments of a particularly venerated lama. The figure on page 40 illustrates some of these boxes.

A libation bowl made from a brass-lined human skull that sits in a triangular metal base. The brass cover is decorated with demon figures, Sanskrit characters, and coral and turquoise. Tibet, 19th to 20th century. H. 26.68 cm., W. 17.78 cm.

Tibetan Buddhist Art

Tibetan Buddhist painting and sculpture are vehicles which best convey the complexity of Lamaism. Painting and sculpture had very specific religious functions. Their creation was usually an act of devotion itself.

Relic boxes worn for protection against evil spirits. Tibet, 19th to 20th century. 2 brass relic boxes on felt strap, 12 × 9 × 4.7 cm. Copper relic box, 8.89 × 7.62 cm. Shrine shaped relic box, silver top and copper back, 6.35 × 5.08 cm.

Amdo men assembled for a formal portrait. Tibet, ca. 1930. Collection of the Newark Museum.

Phurpas, ritual weapons used in exorcism ceremonies. Tibet, 19th to 20th century. R. *Silver phurpa with three demon heads; L. 21.35 cm.* L. *Lacquered wood phurpa with demon head and skulls on top and snakes on the blade; L. 29.21 cm.*

Artists were usually lamas associated with a specific monastery, although some were itinerant. The artist could be commissioned by someone, a layman for example, for a specific occasion; the donor received merit from this commissioning. The event could be the commemoration of a deceased relative, or an offering to a specific deity or for a specific festival. Nepali traders, for example, often donated paintings in Tibet, either to insure the economic success of their mission or to secure the spiritual well-being of their families back in Nepal.

A gilt bronze statue of the goddess Tara. Probably from Nepal, 17th to 18th century. H. 22.86 cm., W. 17.78 cm.

Once created, the paintings and sculpture acquired a deeply religious function. The objects supposedly embodied the mystical energy of the divinities they represented. Individuals meditated upon or prayed to these images and by doing so absorbed the images' spiritual essence and entered into a mystical communion with the deity depicted. An unusual variation of this art were the butter sculptures and tankas made from colored grains, created once for a specific occasion and then destroyed at the conclusion of the ceremony.

All of the tankas and pieces of sculpture found in our collection are small-scale. In the temples and monasteries of Tibet, however, lifesize and larger than lifesize sculpture occupied the altars. In addition, large-scale paintings were also unveiled for special occasions. Very few of these images ever left Tibet and many were destroyed during the past 30 years.

HP

BUDDHISM IN SRI LANKA

Sri Lanka is a beautiful island only 25 miles southeast of India. The narrow strait between the two countries can only be used by small boats, but the southern and eastern harbors have been known for at least 2000 years by sailors from distant parts of the world.

To the Greeks and Romans, the island was Taprobane. The Arabs translated the Sanskrit "Sinhala-divipa" (dwelling-of-lions island) into "Serendib." The Portuguese contracted "Sinhala" into "Cilao," the Dutch made it "Zeilan," and the English gave it one more twist into "Ceylon," which was retained until modern times. Southeast Asians have always known the island as "Lanka."

Legend has it that the island was first colonized in 483 B.C. by Vijaya, a north Indian said to be descended from lions (*sinha*). His group overcame the aborigines (Veddahs) and established the Sinhalese group, whose emblem is still a lion with a sword.

Another legend claims that the Buddha visited Sri Lanka before his death and miraculously left his footprint atop Adan's Peak. The 7353-foot-high mountain and the footprint-shaped depression in the rock are deeply venerated by thousands of devout Buddhists who make the difficult ascent to the site every year.

Closer to historical fact is the mission of Mahinda, who is credited with introducing Buddhism to Sri Lanka in 247 B.C. Mahinda was the son of the Indian emperor Ashoka, the great ruler of the Mauryan empire who converted to Buddhism. Mahinda, fulfilling both his father's wish and a prophecy of the Buddha, went as a missionary to Sri Lanka. According to the *Mahavamsa,* a chronicle compiled in the 5th century A.D. from monastic records going back to the 1st century B.C., Mahinda, stressing the practical kindness and good of Buddhism, converted King Devanampiya Tissa. The king gave a park where Mahinda laid out the plan of a monastery and established the system for monks and teaching. Mahinda's sister brought a branch of the original bodhi tree under which the Buddha had achieved enlightenment, and Ashoka sent a relic, the Buddha's collar bone. This was enshrined in the Thuperama built by King Tissa. Several times rebuilt and restored, it is today a gleaming white bell-shaped stupa with a conical spire and a gilded finial.

Although both Mahayana and Tantric sects existed during the early period of Buddhist history on Sri Lanka, the dominant sect was the Theravadan. The Singhalese, conscious of their role as direct inheritors of the original Buddhism, have always guarded the purity of the doctrine. They have retained the same conservatism toward the image of the Buddha. The artistic canon was fixed in the 2nd century A.D. and continues in an unbroken sequence for centuries. The typical image is herculean in proportion and often monolithic. The preferred pose is a seated one, hands resting in the lap in meditation, all emotion stilled (see above).

One of four huge Buddha images carved on the face of a colossal granite boulder at Gal Vihara, Sri Lanka. They were originally painted or gilded and were protected by an outer shrine attached to the rock in the manner of the Chinese cave temples. Polonnaruva period (12th century A.D.). Photograph by E. Lyons.

Since there was little regard for the image unless it contained a relic, there is not the proliferation of sculptures that one finds in other Buddhist countries, and not many western museums contain a reputable example. The scenes of the Buddha's life or previous lives tend to be painted, not sculpted.

Throughout its long Buddhist history, monks and pilgrims have come to Sri Lanka from other lands to study and review the doctrine preserved in their chronicles written in Pali, and from time to time the island sent out teaching missions. Today, the Singhalese, who make up two-thirds of the population, continue the tradition. A growing project is the Sarvodaya Shramada Movement which has had great success in using the traditional and cultural values of Buddhist philosophy to promote rural village development.

EL

BUDDHISM IN SOUTHEAST ASIA

BURMA

Although the earliest evidence of Buddhism in Burma dates from the 5th century A.D., the first major Buddhist centers are associated with the Pyu, who left Burma's first written records and who are no longer a distinct ethnic group. Seventh and eighth century (Tang period) Chinese sources record that the Pyu capital, Hmawza, on the lower Irrawady River, consisted of a group of seven to eight villages enclosed within a wall of glazed tiles. The people were Buddhists and had 100 richly decorated temples. They used gold and silver crescent-shaped money, wore headdresses adorned with gold flowers and pearls, and they raised rice, grains and sugar cane.

Archaeological evidence supports the Chinese historians. Among the Pyu finds recovered are gold plates inscribed with Buddhist texts, two gold images of Gupta style and a silver gilt casket with an inscription both in Pyu and in a south Indian form of Pali. Within the area were found some bodhisattva images with Mahayana Sanskrit inscriptions, and also some Brahmanical images from a temple built by the Indians for their own use.

There was another group of early inhabitants farther south at Thaton, a little north of Rangoon. The Mons, who were also in Thailand, had their capital first at Thaton and then at Pegu. Both places were once sea ports (remains of foreign ships have been uncovered), but both are now inland. They called their land Ramannadesa, and according to the type of stupa remains and the few images of Gupta style, they must have embraced Theravada Buddhism at about the same time as their relatives in Thailand.

What we know of Pyu and Mon early history is typical for Southeast Asia. From the Indian trading posts, missionaries spread the Buddhist doctrine, while Brahmins instructed the rulers in court ritual. The influence of both sects was lasting.

There was one group in the north of Burma that does not fit the Theravada-Brahmin picture. The Ari sect developed from Tibetan Buddhism. The monks were bearded, had long hair, wore blue-black robes, fought and drank. Their religion included Naga (water serpent spirit) worship, Sakti wives (consorts of Hindu gods who symbolized the gods' active, energetic aspect) for the Buddha, magic and a debased Mahayana canon in Sanskrit. They are not quite extinct today, but were crushed as a cult in the 11th century when they were banished from Pagan.

Wooden figures of two Nats, ghosts or spirits of legendary heroes. Burma, 19th century. L. *H. 113.03 cm.* R. *H. 99.06 cm.*

Pagan, originally a cluster of 19 Burmese villages near the confluence of the Irrawady and Chindwin rivers, was enclosed by a wall in A.D. 849, but it did not become important until the 11th century when its inhabitants came under a strong ruler, Anawrahta (1044–77).

Anawrahta met and was deeply impressed by Shin Arahan, a Mon Buddhist monk, and with the king's encouragement, Buddhism spread rapidly. The Burmese also adopted the Mon alphabet to write their own language. Apparently wishing to assist Shin Arahan's teaching, Anawrahta asked the king of Thaton, Manuka, for monks and copies of the scriptures. When the king refused, Anawrahta simply called up the troops, marched to Thaton and took everything—monks, scriptures, images, craftsmen, wealth and the king himself—and thus began the two centuries of temple building that makes Pagan unique in the world.

The 16 square miles of the Pagan area is a sea of 5,000 temples and stupas, a sunbaked plain more crowded with brick and stone than the famous "stone

The Mahabodi temple, Burma, that was modeled after the Bodh Gaya temple in India. 13th century. Photograph by E. Lyons.

forest" of Angkor Wat in Cambodia. Shining with new whitewash and gilt, or crumbling into ruins beyond repair, they divide roughly into two general types: those built by Mon artisans or following their pattern, and those built by the Burmese, often after Indian models (see above).

There are rarely any remains of the buildings for the monks and the congregation that would surround the temple, nor any trace of secular buildings, nor the great palace built by King Kyanzittha. They would have been of wood, bamboo, and thatch, an easy and economical type of construction and one suited to a tropical climate.

In 1287 Pagan was captured by the Mongols. The king and court fled; the government of upper Burma was taken over by Shan chiefs who gave token allegiance to the Emperor of China.

The Burmese continued to build temples, both in villages and in the successive capitals of their increasingly ineffective kings. Probably the best known in the present day is the glittering Shwedagon in Rangoon. It was begun as a relic chamber to enshrine the hairs of the Buddha at an early time when Rangoon was a small village. Built over the small chamber were several structures of stone and brick which reached a height of 27 feet, but the building did not stop. In 1363 the pagoda had reached 66 feet, and had been at least twice completely gilded. It is now 326 feet high, comprising a bell on a square plinth surmounted by a spire shaped like a bud and topped by a *hti* (umbrella) studded with precious stones (gems and personal jewelry donated by the devout in the late 1960s). Today, the temples of Pagan are historical monuments more under the care of the Archaeological Service and the Tourist Bureau than the Sangha, although monks are present.

The living heart of Buddhism in Southeast Asia lies in the village or city community temple or *wat.* In general, the main structure is a large hall covered with wooden overlapping roofs. Inside, opposite the entrance is a platform for the monks to sit on; behind this is an altar and an image of the Buddha often flanked by small shrines, chests for religious texts, vases of flowers, fans, umbrellas. The walls may be painted with murals on Buddhist themes and are usually overlaid with religious lithographs, calendars and horoscopes. If the temple is flourishing, there will be a dormitory building or individual cells for the monks. Otherwise, they sleep on mats in the hall in front of the image. Kitchen and bathing areas are separate. The buildings should be in a pleasant, tree-shaded area surrounded by a fence or a wall to mark the division between the spiritual and the worldly. Whoever enters the sacred precinct must do so respectfully, and barefoot.

In Burma, Thailand, Laos and Cambodia, a man is considered an incomplete being until he has taken vows and been directly part of the religious life for some length of time, be it days or years. A boy can become a novice at the age of twelve, but to become a

Seated Buddha of wood, heavily gilded and decorated with paste jewels. The Buddha's hand stretches over his knee to touch the earth and call it to witness his victory over evil. Burma, 19th century. H. 43.18 cm.

monk he must be twenty years old, have the permission of his parents, be of sound mind and body and without debts or criminal record.

Monks and novices conform to the traditional and strict rules. They wear standard yellow robes and may own only the barest necessities, such as a razor, towel, food bowl, and umbrella. They do not "beg"; they silently accept whatever food is offered and they may not eat after midday until the next dawn. They do not handle money, they are forbidden sex, perfume, dancing, jewelry and soft beds. They live in simple bare cells, and spend most of the time in study, reciting passages learned from the texts, and meditation.

The average day of a monk's life is like this. He begins his day at first dawn, between 5:30 and 6:00 a.m., when he gathers with the others for a kind of roll call, a renewal of his pledge, and prayers. After that, the novices do chores while the monks meditate until breakfast. Around 7:30 they file out to collect food from the neighborhood households, silently accepting whatever is put in the bowl. The donor does not expect to be thanked as it is he who gains the merit by his giving.

The original rule was that the monk must mix the contents of his bowl and eat, no matter the taste. Today, however, a layman takes over and manages with the donations to provide a good, cooked meal at noon, the last food the monk will eat until the next day's breakfast.

In the afternoon, the monks may teach, study, meditate. They may leave the temple for a walk, a talk with the villagers, but must be back by sundown, around 6:00 p.m. A little later, they gather in front of the Buddha image for a sermon and to chant and recite passages memorized from the sutras before retiring for the night.

It is a plain life, but not uncomfortable and not isolated. The wat is the center of the community. People come in to ask for advice, to sit in the cool, shaded *sala* (pavillion) exchanging news and gossip, and to invite the monks to preside at numerous ceremonies, everything from a cremation to blessing a new truck. The strict Buddhist admits these rites cannot be found in the sutras, but is reassured by them anyway.

There is no pressure to remain a monk for life, and whether he stays a short or a long time, he has had firsthand contact with the roots of his native beliefs and culture, a form of universal religious training. He has also been part of a democratic community in which his worldly rank or wealth gives no privileges.

The small number of lifetime monks and the ever-renewing community of monks within the temple, plus the direct experience of a large part of the male population in Burma, Thailand, Laos, Cambodia and Sri Lanka is a major factor in keeping the Theravada doctrine an alive and vital force.

Perhaps we should note that women are not excluded from the Buddhist life. There are temple communities of white-robed nuns who follow the same precepts and rules as the monks. Yet, there is not the same degree of social approval. Most women prefer to support their local temple by providing food, etc., and regard the nunnery as a refuge for those women without a family to care for them.

EL

THAILAND

Thailand was one of the earliest regions outside India to adopt the Buddhist religion. There is a persistent legend that it came through two missionaries, Sona and Utara, sent by India's great King Ashoka about the same time as his son Mahinda went on a similar mission to Sri Lanka. If there is no genuine evidence for this early date (3rd century B.C.), we do know that contact with India had been established by the first century A.D. Excavations at the site of Chansen produced

Elephant tusk completely carved with figures of the Buddha that, with a matching tusk, would have been placed on a temple altar. Burma, 18th century. L. 76 cm.

Religious manuscript on tree bark paper that recounts stories of the ten previous births of the Buddha. The illustration depicts the virtue of perseverance. Thailand, 19th century. L. 67.31 cm., H. (of page) 13.97 cm.

an Indian ivory comb engraved with Buddhist symbols from a stratum dated by C14 to the 1st century, and at U'Thong, seals and jewelry similar to those from 2nd–4th century A.D. Oc-eo were found. (Oc-eo is a Cambodian site believed to be associated with Funan, an ancient Southeast Asian center.)

The greatest gap in Thailand's history is between the end of the prehistoric era (ca. A.D. 100) and the appearance of Buddha images in the Dvaravati period (6th?–11th centuries A.D.). But even the Dvaravati period eludes us. We know only from the Chinese records and a few excavated seals inscribed "King of Dvaravati" that the kingdom existed; we do not know when it began or where its capital lay.

But by the 7th century, images were being produced by Dvaravati sculptors in the style of 3rd–6th century A.D. India. The prototype is the extremely beautiful, slim and radiant figure of the great Gupta age. Never having seen the original, however, and having as models only the figurines or small clay votive tablets brought by the Indian teachers, the sculptor often had to invent details, especially when he translated a relief into full round. By and large the sculptors followed the iconographic rules, but gave their images the Mon features of the local people. The face is more square and boyish than the Indian, the eyebrows are joined over slightly bulging eyes, the nose is a bit snub, the mouth is large but sensitive with a gentle smile. One can see the relationship, but it is that of a cousin in a large family.

Perhaps it was this kind of invention or misunderstanding that produced some images that have no counterpart in India. The usual Dvaravati Buddha has both hands raised to shoulder height, palms out, the first finger and thumb joined in a gesture meaning exposition or explaining the doctrine. In India, only one hand is in this position, and the figure is nearly always seated. (One likes to imagine that the only model had lost a hand or arm so the sculptor duplicated the remaining one. The result was logical enough and the style was repeated.)

The Khmer empire of Cambodia grew strong in the 10th century and in the 11th spread like a slow but powerful flood into central and northeastern Thailand. King Suryavarman I established his control as far as Lopburi and his influence beyond that. Khmer governors took over the administration, built temples to Khmer specifications and filled them with images, usually Hindu. Yet even when the court was Hindu, the majority of the local population remained Buddhist. The Buddhist images of the time follow the Khmer fashion and appear more severe and more masculine than the earlier Dvaravati style.

The first truly *Thai* period is the Sukhothai of the 13th–15th centuries. The Thais, a non-Chinese group with a homeland in southern China, had long been filtering south into Laos, Burma and the Menam valley (in Thailand). By the 13th century, they were strong enough to overthrow the Khmer administration and set up their own kingdom with a capital at Sukhothai.

They had already been converted to Buddhism, and with the conviction of new converts they regarded the contemporary Buddhist teaching as confused and impure, contaminated by the Khmer intrusion of Brahminism and Mahayana elements. To purify it they invited monks from Sri Lanka to come with copies of the original texts and to instruct and reordain the Thai monks.

They may also have attempted to make the image more "correct" by making it more closely conform to the *silpa sastra* rules, the 33 major and 80 minor marks identifying a superior and spiritual being. Certainly the Sukhothai image exhibits a sharp break from the square, realistic Khmer style. The head is egg shaped, the eyebrows arch like a bow (see below), the torso is leonine, the graceful arms reach to the knees, the fingers are webbed, the heels protrude. If the sculptor followed the iconographic rules too faithfully the result could be close to absurdity, but many succeeded in creating a radiant being formed of subtly rhythmical curves and volumes with the flow and energy of a flame.

From the mid-15th to the mid-18th centuries, the Thai capital shifted to Ayutthaya (40 miles north of Bangkok), a city of temples and wealth and larger than London at the time. In the 17th century, Ayutthaya was well known to Europe, and the Portuguese, Dutch, French and British all made more or less serious attempts at domination. With extraordinary diplomacy, the Thai kings played one country against another and somehow managed to keep pleasant relations with everyone while maintaining their own national freedom.

Bronze head of the Buddha. Thailand, Sukhothai period (13th to 15th century A.D.). H. 20.32 cm.

Stone head of the Buddha. Thailand, Ayutthaya period (16th century A.D.). H. 37.85 cm.

Ayutthaya was sacked and burned by the Burmese in 1767. The destruction was enormous; the city could not be rebuilt. The Thais recovered and set out to recreate Ayutthaya in Bangkok. The city plan was the same, temples of the same design were built, but few new images were made for them. Older images were retrieved from the ruins, restored and reinstalled in their new sanctuaries.

It was in the temple murals that a creative spirit emerged. The walls of nearly every temple were painted with scenes from the life of the Buddha, surrounding the gilded image with glowing color. They were intended as visual aids to a largely illiterate public; each scene could remind the viewer of an episode in the Buddha's life or previous lives and its implicit moral message.

Gilt bronze Buddha in "royal attire" or the rich robes of a Universal King, the moral leader of mankind. Thailand, 18th to 19th century. H. 69.85 cm.

Buddhism is a living religion for over 90% of Thais. As in Burma, a man is not considered "complete" until he has spent some time in the monastic life. (Few women become nuns.) Only a few remain for life and they form the core of the religion's administration which has a form almost parallel to that of the civil government. There is a Supreme Patriarch nominated by the Ecclesiastical Council and appointed by the king. The church council, like the civil council of ministers, has dignitaries in charge of administration, education, etc., under a presiding officer who is a clerical Prime Minister. There is a General Assembly equivalent in role to the National Assembly and district or diocesan officials comparable to secular government officers who carry out church business in the provinces. It is a system much more tightly organized than in Burma and Sri Lanka, the other major Theravada countries.

There are two main sects in Thailand today, the Mahanikaya and the Dammayutika, which are not very different as far as the congregation is concerned. The Dammayutika was founded in the mid 19th century by King Mongut who felt the monks had become a little too worldly and easy going. This sect is more austere than the Mahanikaya sect, and the monks interpret the traditional rules of the Sangha more closely. They are also more concerned with the education of monks. At Mohamakuta (Great Mongut) University, monks of both sects can study English and western philosophy, along with Pali and Buddhist subjects.

EL

LAOS

The small nation of Laos is landlocked by its surrounding neighbors, Thailand, Burma, China, Vietnam and Cambodia. Obviously, much of its history, politics, composition of its population, its religion and culture stem from this crossroads position.

The early history of the area is obscure. Its history as an independent state does not clearly exist until the 14th century when the kingdom of LanXang was established by Fa Ngum (1353–1373). Prior to this time, the area was under the influence of either the Mons or the Khmers.

LanXang had a capital at Vientiene and another farther north at Luang Prabang. Fa Ngum is credited with introducing Theravada Buddhism, with himself as protector of the religion and under the protection of the Buddha. An image, the Phra Bang, which was said to have come from Sri Lanka, was sent to him by the king of Cambodia and became the revered state icon.

Modern history begins in 1563 when King Saya Setthathirat, a prince from Chiangmai, Thailand, moved to Vientiene after being ousted by the Burmese. He brought with him a precious image, the Emerald Buddha, and built a temple for it, Wat Phra Keo

(Temple of the Green Emerald Buddha). This is the same image, the palladium of the Thai Empire, housed today in a temple of the same name in Bangkok. It was taken from Laos in 1778 by Rama I on the grounds that it rightfully belonged to the Thai, and had been illegally removed from Chiangmai.

At the same time (mid 16th century), Laos was divided into three districts, Vientiene in the west, Luang Prabang in the north and Champassak in the south bordering Cambodia. From then on, Laos was more or less a Thai province. In 1901, Laos became a French protectorate, and in 1948 achieved a few decades of independence before falling behind the bamboo curtain of Vietnam.

Until recently, the Lao culture may be interpreted as a provincial version of the Thai. As in Thailand and Burma, the wat constitutes the center and pride of the community; it is usually built completely by local workmen and with local funds. Except in the north where the temples took on a strong Burmese influence, the Lao wat followed the Thai style of a brick and stucco rectangle, a columned portico with balustrades and carved wooden doors.

Stone corner architectural element carved on two sides with a figure of the seated Buddha. Mon-Khmer, Thailand; 8th to 12th century. H. 32.5 m.

Northern Thai village Buddhist monk and child. The wat (temple) functions as a local community center. Spiritual advice or practical help is offered by the monks to those of all ages. Photograph by E. Lyons.

The wat normally has a mixed collection of Buddhist images, an occasional provincial Mon or Khmer type rescued from abandoned ruins, or perhaps one of the rare 14th–15th century bronzes, as delicate and graceful as their Thai Sukhothai period cousins, but the majority are 18th–19th century images, distinctively Lao. The typical Lao image has a stiff and rigid pose, the features are as sharply cut as a woodcarving, the nose long and rigid, the mouth small, the eyes often inlaid with glass or shell.

The numerous festivals marking events of the Buddha's life that are celebrated during the calender year are not unique to Laos, but the public support and enthusiasm for these ceremonies are. Nearly every month has something to be celebrated. In January the temples are decorated and the monks recite and dramatize the Vessantara Jataka, the last story of the Buddha's previous births. February is the anniversary of the meeting of the disciples at which the Buddha gave the rules of the doctrine and predicted his own death. In May, his birth, enlightenment and death, which occurred on the same day of the same month, are commemorated. July brings the cleaning of temples, the beginning of Buddhist Lent and three months of retreat for monks. In October and November, the people obtain merit with offerings to temples and monks. November also has the fete of That Loung, the national pagoda, and homage is paid to the enshrined relic.

Not strictly of Buddhist origin but always involving monks and temples are other events. In June there is a kind of rowdy festival during which big rockets are exploded to mark the end of the dry season and call forth the rain. Boat races are held in October, and

(Continued on page 57)

Below
Musicial instruments which accompanied rituals of Tibetan Buddhism in the temple. 19th to 20th century. Clockwise from top: Long collapsible trumpets of copper and brass; L. open 2.3 m., closed 1 m. Drum made from two skin-covered brain pans; H. 12.7 cm., D. 17.78 cm. Brass cymbals used in temple orchestras; D. 30.48 cm. Trumpet made from a human thigh bone, with brass on the top and bottom; L. 33.02 cm. Drum made from two small skin-covered skull caps, with two small beaters attached with a silk strap; L. 71.12 cm., D. 10.79 cm. Skin-covered wood drum, with cowrie shells and tassels; H. 9.9 cm., D. 19.55 cm.

page 51
Tanka depicting Amitayus Buddha with Tara of the Seven Eyes (lower right) and the god Ushnishavijaya (lower left). Tibet, 18th century. Painted cloth. 1.9 m. × 1.09 m.

page 52
Tanka showing Lha-mo riding her mule over a sea of blood. Tibet, 18th century. Painted cloth. 85 × 45 cm.

page 53
The goddess Tara seated on the lap of the god Palkhorlodompa. Probably from Nepal, 17th to 18th century. Gilt bronze. H. 21.95 cm., W. 12.70.

page 54
Gilt bronze Maitreya. China, Eastern Wei period (A.D. 536). H. 60.96 cm.

page 55
Two monks sitting by the altar in the main hall of Yuan Tong Si Temple, Kunming, Yunnan, China. Photograph by H. Peters.

page 56
Wooden model of the facade of a temple or shrine. A tiny image or painting would be revealed by opening the door. Burma, 18th to 19th century. H. 87.63 cm., W. 59.53 cm.

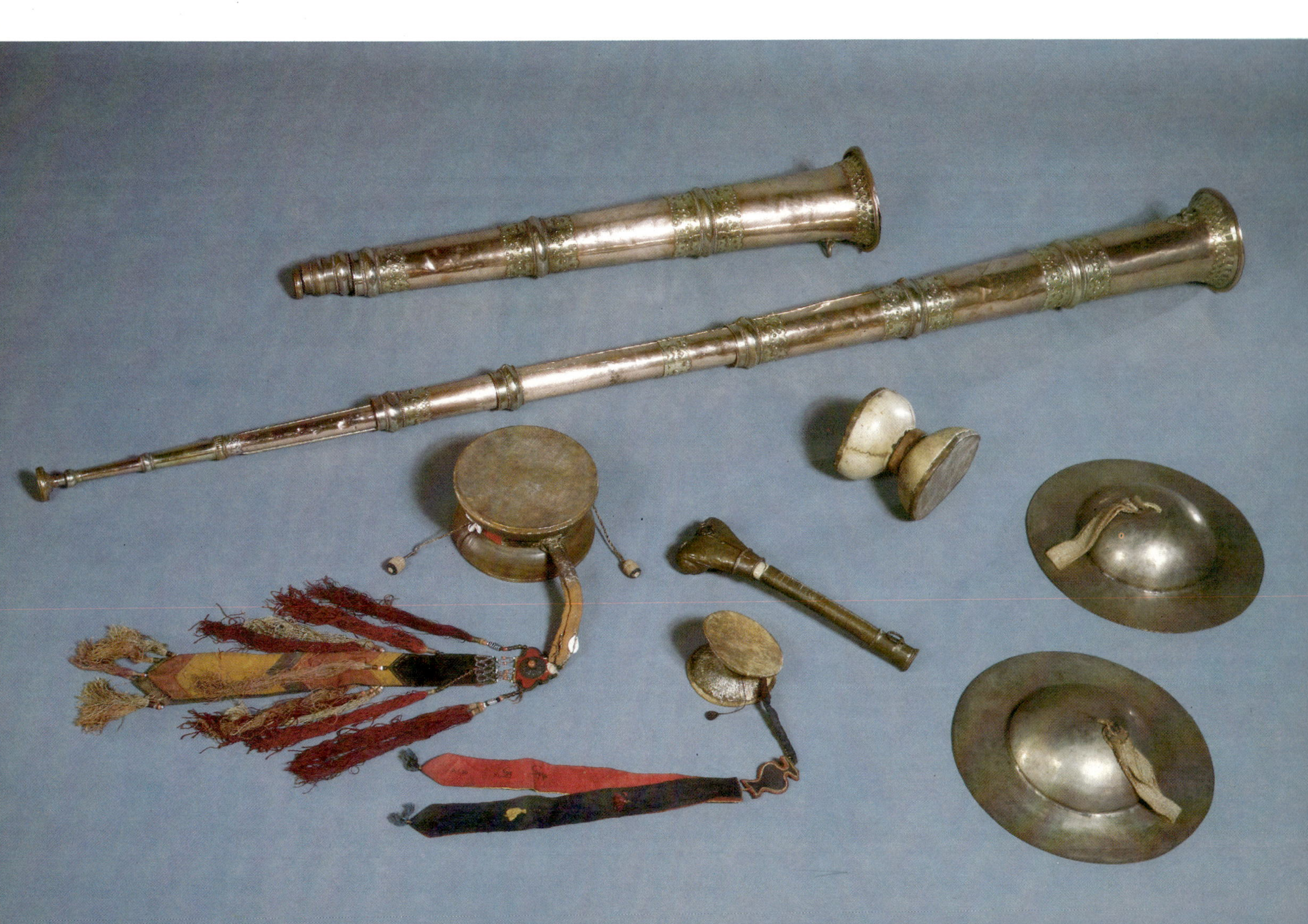

there is always a temple fair to be found somewhere in the country.

Buddhism has always been at the core of Lao life and is considered a blessing to be celebrated joyously as well as solemnly.

EL

CAMBODIA

Sanskrit inscriptions refer to the inhabitants of modern Cambodia as Kambuja and the country as Kambujadesa; the Cham, central Vietnam neighbors, and the 9th century Arab traders called the people Khmer. The Europeans used variations on Kambuja—Camboxa, Cambodge. . . . Cambodia. The recent revolutionary "Khmer Rouge" coined "Kampuchea" for the land they devastated.

The earliest empire, Funan, developed in the center and the delta country. Probably already established for a century or two, it was visited in the 3rd century A.D. by Chinese envoys who described the richly decorated palace of the king. From records and some associated excavated material, Funan seems to have been more Hindu than Buddhist.

The technical skills for irrigation, engineering and architecture were passed on, and the political system, or the Hindu ceremonial aspect of it, was adopted by local rulers. By and large, the succeeding Khmer kings from the 7th to the 12th century built their monuments to honor the Hindu gods Shiva or Vishnu. Yet, Chinese texts as early as the 4th century list a considerable number of Buddhist images sent as gifts from Funan to China. Also, two Buddhist monks from early Funan went to China and translated Sanskrit texts into Chinese.

Buddhism had greater appeal to the masses than did the Hindu religion. The Buddhist message of compassion, love, non-violence and self-accountability was easy to understand. Also, unlike the caste system practiced by Hindus, in Buddhism birth did not automatically lock an individual into a low stratum of society.

Most probably, the Buddhist temples were of wood (stone was scarce in the delta region), and wood cannot long endure in a tropical climate. (Some stone foundations have been found, but little is known of pre-modern Buddhist architecture.) Only a few early Buddhist images are known; among them are three rare and quite beautiful wooden standing figures of Gupta style which were preserved in a marsh. These few may be representative of a large number. There is also a stone head and two stone standing Buddhas of post-Gupta, 6th century style, which were found at Wat Romlok. They are already in a local style.

After the 6th century, the spice and silk route was interrupted. There are hardly any references to Southeast Asia in Indian literature and history of this period.

Temple in Petburi, Thailand. 18th century. The multiple overlapping roofs are a distinctive characteristic of Thai temple architecture. Photograph by E. Lyons.

Cambodia, with its own creative genius, now begins a socio-economic revolution that will produce the power and glory of Angkor. That period of greatness still inspires every Cambodian, and throughout times of peace or trouble to the present day, the towers of Angkor Wat have been on the flag of every ruler as a national symbol. It is impossible to discuss any aspect of Cambodia, historical, religious, economic or ethnological, without some knowledge of Angkor.

In the 9th century, the Khmer kings established their capitals in the Angkor region. It was a good central site with alluvial soil, rivers and a lake full of fish. Here they built their temples and around them created a network of main supply channels, dikes and reservoirs to collect, store and redistribute water that would make the earth yield two or three crops a year. For more than two centuries, temple after temple, with its necessary reservoirs and canals, opened more land for cultivation and ensured the empire's prosperity.

The temples reflect the combination of Hinduism and Buddhism that characterizes Cambodian thought at the time. Although no two temples are alike, each is essentially a storied central tower on a square, surrounded by walls and terraces with secondary towers. The larger ones include palaces and offices within the walled compounds, and the whole can be seen as a complex microcosmos, with a horizontal and vertical axis. The moats are the oceans surrounding the series of worlds represented by the tiers of terraces. The central temple symbolizes Mount Meru (in Hindu cosmology, the center of the universe and home of the gods), with its five peaks; its inner sanctuary is both the dwelling place of the god and an altar to fertility.

Angkor Wat is the greatest and best known of these temples. Built by Suryavarman II between A.D. 1113 and 1150, the basic area is a rectangle 1,300 by 1,500 meters, surrounded by a moat 2½ miles in circumference. The central mass with a large tower is surrounded by three concentric galleries reached by avenues through two external enclosures. Smaller towers, 12 in all, rise from the inner galleries. After the outer gallery with its half mile of superbly carved reliefs of chariots, noble kings and armies from the Mahabharata and the Ramayana, the visitor can wander for hours in and out of rooms, courtyards and galleries, constantly surprised by vistas or walls carved with floral designs or figures, including the lovely dancing *apsaras,* the heavenly chorus girls.

But the very glory of Angkor created disaster. There was too much building and too little maintenance of the hydraulic network. The area of productive land diminished. In 1177, the Chams of central Vietnam attacked and sacked Angkor before they were driven out.

Jayavarman VII (1181–1219) assumed the leadership of a dispirited country. This most powerful king, who managed to hold off disaster for several years, recognized the gulf between the people and the court. Converting to a kind of mystical Buddhism, he put his land under the protection of the Buddha and declared in an inscription, "It is the unhappiness of the people which makes the King unhappy and not his own private sorrows."

He covered the country with Buddhist temples and with a chain of hostels and hospitals that stretched over the mountains into Thailand. But he did not completely give up the old royal traditions. He built his own capital next to Angkor Wat and placed a temple-mausoleum in its center, and from its 54 towers the gigantic face of Jayavarman transformed or melded into Buddha as Universal King looks over the whole compound with a slight smile, both compassionate and enigmatic.

Jayavarman's reign is the last of the power and greatness of the Khmer empire. The Thais throw off the Khmer colonial administration and invade Cambodia again and again until they destroy the capital cities and take home as captives many trained officials, craftsmen and ballet dancers.

In 1431, the court and the decimated, impoverished population abandoned Angkor to the jungle and moved south to the Phnom Penh area. After the move to Phnom Penh, the country turned to a simple subsistence economy of individual effort with little interference or demands from the government. Small villages clustered around a Buddhist temple, the only real center of organization and civilization.

The French colonial administration which took over in the 1860s supported the Buddhist organizations, built a Buddhist college and library, expanded educational and economic opportunities, but made little change in the general social fabric. Perhaps there should have been more changes to create a wealthy, modern society. The international communist revolution movement made some passionate converts within the country who believed that a great Cambodian society could only be formed by abolishing all institutions and "tainted" members of the present and making a completely new beginning. The Khmer Rouge madness killed nearly 3 million people, and destroyed hundreds of village schools and temples. The present situation is still unhappy and the future uncertain, but Angkor Wat is again a Buddhist sanctuary.

EL

VIETNAM

Vietnam was originally three separate areas of more or less different ethnic groups. Early Chinese and Southeast Asian records give different names to the areas, and until the end of French domination after World War II, the north was known as Tonkin, the center as Annam, and the southern tip, the Mekong delta, as Cochin China.

A doorway of the great temple of Angkor Wat, Cambodia. A.D. 1113–1150. Angkor Wat was originally Hindu. It became a Buddhist sanctuary in the 15th century and remains as one today. Photograph by E. Lyons.

Large bronze image of the Buddha. Found at Dong doung, Annam, Vietnam, but originally from either the Amaravati coast of India or Sri Lanka. 4th century A.D.

Its history is extremely complicated. Around 111 B.C., the Chinese conquered and annexed a large part of the north. In spite of constant rebellion and some periods of independence, it remained a Chinese province until A.D. 938, organized in Chinese fashion, with Chinese as the official language. The center of the long, narrow country was occupied by the Chams, a coastal and seafaring people who devoted a large part of their immense energy to piracy and warfare. The southern section of the country, the Mekong delta area, included the 2nd century early Cambodian port of Oc-eo (near Saigon) which when excavated yielded Roman coins, Sassanian seals and other evidence of international trade.

The religious history of Vietnam is as mixed as its political story. Tonkin, north Vietnam, was an early center of Buddhist activity. The coastline offered welcome ports for sailors and monks from India, and the area was also a first stage for the stream of Chinese pilgrims going to India. Among the religious centers was a school of Dhyana Buddhism founded at Bac-ninh around A.D. 580. None of these centers are dated to later than the 6th century when world conditions cut off trade and the Indian presence vanished. North Vietnam, under strong Chinese influence, drifted back largely to a worship of guardian nature spirits and a vague Confucianism.

Champa, central Vietnam, became a Buddhist center, particularly under Indravarman II (A.D. 875–898), a fervent Buddhist patron. Until the end of the 11th century, the Chams produced a style of religious architecture and sculpture, combining both Buddhist and Hindu elements, that was highly individual. They built powerful brick towers with elaborately decorated lintels and carved images that were sometimes of a sensitive beauty and as often of brutal vigor, expressing their own untamed vitality. However, the Chams' energy was not inexhaustible, and the constant fighting finally reduced them to insignificance. Only a small number exist today.

Buddhism in recent times has divided into several sects, some Mahayana, some Theravada, some owing little to the original doctrine and acting on radical and political principles. Some Vietnamese adopted Catholicism during the French period, although not giving up Confucian ancestor rituals. Information on the attitude of the current government toward any form of religion is contradictory. Apparently it is not totally banned, but it is not encouraged.

EL

INDONESIA

By A.D. 650, the Sivijaya Empire, believed by many scholars to be based somewhere in Sumatra, was an important naval and commercial power extending its influence from southern Thailand to central Java. It was also a center of Buddhist learning, and a way station between India and China. I Jing, the Chinese Buddhist monk, made lengthy visits there in circa A.D. 671, 687 and 693. He reported there were 1,000 monks and that he had translated and taken back to China 400 sacred texts.

For a time, there were smaller dynasties in Java which were both Hindu and Mahayana Buddhist. The Dieng plateau has several Shivaist Hindu temples dating to the 8th century and later, while in Java, the Kalasan temple was dedicated to Tara, a Buddhist Tantric goddess, in A.D. 778. But the great masterpiece is Borobudur, the most important Buddhist monument in Southeast Asia.

From a distance, Borobudur has the shape of a stupa, combining the ancient symbols of earth (square) and heaven (circle) with a base of five square, walled terraces followed by three circular platforms. Four stairways go from bottom to top. There is no inner space except for one small chamber inside the closed pinnacle. The whole monument is literally a stone covered hill that rises out of the plain like a volcano. Two million cubic feet of stone had to be cut, transported, laid in place and carved. There are 27,000 square feet of carved surfaces and 504 Buddha images.

Borobudur is a mandala of the Buddhist world, a visible representation of the doctrine. For the pilgrim circling the monument, the long physical climb symbolizes the spiritual journey from the depths of earthly existence to the heavenly void.

Each stage has an equivalent and a reminder in the relief carvings. The base depicts crowded scenes of earthly life, household work, feasting, gambling, etc. This initial tier was originally covered, probably as a symbol of what the pilgrim put behind him when he began his journey to salvation.

As he climbs upward, the style of the reliefs changes to reflect his spiritual progress; the crowded scenes become more formal and ordered, the realistic figures become more idealized. There is also a chronological progression in the theme of the reliefs. Those on the inner wall of the terrace balustrades depict the Jatakas, the previous births of the Buddha; the monument walls are carved with scenes from the life of Sakyamuni, the historical Buddha, followed by Maitreya, the Buddha to come, and the story of Prince Suddhana, who became a bodhisattva and who visited ascetics, sages, monks and sacred places in the quest for enlightenment. Finally, on the last square terrace, in stylized, hieratic scenes, is Samantabhadra, the very last Buddha of the future.

Higher again are the three open circular platforms ringed with 72 smaller stupas, each containing a Buddha image. The number has a significance as every 72 years there is a change of one degree in the procession of the equinox, thus the 72 images represent the Buddhist law for all past and future time.

Relief from the Borobudur stupa, Indonesia. 9th century A.D. On five walled square terraces there are 27,000 square feet of carvings depicting the Buddhist story. Photograph by E. Lyons.

The pilgrim who has reached the top of the monument has figuratively passed through the three main stages of life, from the sphere of desire (the base) and the sphere of form (terraces) to the sphere of formlessness (open platforms). And when he stands at the top surrounded only by sky and space, he faces the Void, but is still tied to life and the final truth is not disclosed. The crowning pinnacle is solid, revealing nothing.

This great Mahayana Buddhist monument with its classic Indonesian-Gupta reliefs and its serene and gentle images is the last purely Buddhist structure in Java, and close to the end of monumental art and architecture in central Java. The religious and government centers were moved to east Java by A.D. 915, and Hinduism became the predominant faith. In the late 13th century, the Islamic religion, largely introduced by Moslems from India, makes some converts, and by the 16th century its followers constitute the majority. The periods of Portuguese and Dutch domination are responsible for the small minority of Catholics and Protestants, and although barely evident in the statistics, a number of Buddhists are active.

The Indonesian state regards the Borobudur as an important part of their cultural heritage, carefully protects it, and with the help of UNESCO has just completed a decade's work of conservation and restoration.

EL

BIBLIOGRAPHY

GENERAL

Bechert, Heinz, and Richard Gombrich
1984 *The World of Buddhism.* New York: Facts on File Publications.

Conze, Edward
1965 *Buddhism: Its Essence and Development.* New York: Harper and Row.

Gard, Richard
1961 *Buddhism.* New York: Washington Square Press.

Rice, Talbot Tamara
1965 *Ancient Arts of Central Asia.* New York: Frederick A. Prager, Inc.

Robinson, Richard H.
1960 *The Buddhist Religion.* Belmont: Dickenson Co.

Saunders, Dale E.
1960 *Mudras.* New York: Pantheon Books Inc.

Seckel, Dietrich
1964 *The Art of Buddhism.* New York: Crown Publishers, Inc.

INDIA

Basham, A. L.
1959 *The Wonder That Was India.* New York: Grove Press.

Dutt, Sukumar
1962 *Buddhist Monks and Monasteries of India.* London: George Allen and Unwin Ltd.

Rowland, Benjamin
1953 *The Art and Architecture of India.* Baltimore: Penguin Books.

CHINA

Ch'en, Kenneth
1964 *Buddhism in China,* A Historical Survey. Princeton: Princeton University Press.

Davidson, J. Leroy
1955 *The Lotus Sutra in Chinese Art; A Study in Buddhist Art to the Year 1000.* New Haven: Yale University Press.

Gray, Basil
1959 *Buddhist Cave Paintings at Tun-Huang.* London: Faber and Faber.

Sickman, Lawrence, and Alexander Soper
1971 *The Art and Architecture of China.* Baltimore: Penguin Books.

Siren, Osvald
1925 *Chinese Sculpture from the 5th to the 14th Century.* New York: Scribner.

Wright, Arthur
1959 *Buddhism in Chinese History.* Stanford: Stanford University Press.

TIBET-NEPAL

Olson, Eleanor
1950 *Catalogue of the Tibetan Collection and Other Lamaist Articles in the Newark Museum.* Newark: Newark Museum.

Pal, Pratapaditya
1969 *The Art of Tibet.* New York: Asia House Gallery.
1975 *Nepal Where the Gods Are Young.* New York: Asia House Gallery.

Reynolds, Valrae
1978 *Tibet, A Lost World.* New York: The American Federation of Arts.

Reynolds, Valrae, and Amy Heller
1983 *Tibetan Collection,* catalogue introduction. Newark: Newark Museum.

Tucci, Guiseppe
1970 *The Religions of Tibet.* Trans. Geoffrey Samuel. Berkeley: University of California Press.

JAPAN

Embree, John F.
1969 *Suye Mura.* Chicago: The University of Chicago Press.

Kyotaro, Nishi Kawa, and Emily J. Soro
1982 *Japanese Buddhist Sculpture.* Catalogue. Fort Worth: Kimball Art Museum.

Paine, Robert, and Alexander Soper
1981 *The Art and Architecture of Japan.* New York: Penguin Books.

Sanson, G. B.
1943 *Japan, A Short Cultural History.* New York: Appleton-Century-Crofts.

Saunders, Dale
1964 *Buddhism in Japan.* Philadelphia: University of Pennsylvania Press.

SOUTHEAST ASIA

Bernet Kempers, A. J.
1959 *Ancient Indonesian Art.* Cambridge, MA: Harvard University Press.

Briggs, L. P.
1959 *The Ancient Khmer Empire.* Philadelphia: American Philosophical Society.

Dumarcay, J.
1978 *Borobudur.* Kuala Lumpur: Oxford University Press.

Fontein, J.
1971 *Ancient Indonesian Art.* New York: Asia Society.

Luce, G. H.
1969-70 *Old Burma, Early Pagan.* New York: J. J. Augustin.

Rajavaramuni, Phra
1984 *Thai Buddhism in the Buddhist World.* Bangkok: Mahachulalongkorn Buddhist University.

Spiro, Melford
1970 *Buddhism and Society: A Great Tradition and Its Burmese Vicissitudes.* New York: Harper & Row.

Swearer, Donald K.
1981 *Buddhism and Society in Southeast Asia.* Chambersberg, PA: Anima Books.

Tambiah, Stanley
1984 *The Buddhist Saints of the Forest and the Cult of Amulets.* Cambridge: Cambridge University Press.

GLOSSARY

Arhat (Sanskrit)—An individual who has extinguished all desires and attained enlightenment through his own efforts.

Avalokitesvara (Sanskrit; Chinese: Guanyin; Japanese: Kannon)—The bodhisattva of goodness and compassion.

Bodhi (Sanskrit)—Enlightenment.

Bodhi Tree—The tree under which the Buddha attained enlightenment, or a tree supposedly descended from that tree.

Bodhisattva (Sanskrit)—In Theravada Buddhism the term refers to the Buddha in his various earthly forms. In Mahayana Buddhism the term refers to an enlightened being on his way to Buddhahood but who postpones his goal to keep a vow to help all life attain salvation.

Buddha—An enlightened being; particularly used for the historical founder of Buddhism, Gautama Buddha.

Caitya (Sanskrit)—A cult of sacred locations based on mid-first millennium B.C. northern Indian belief that certain locations were the abode of special spirits. The term now is generally synonymous with stupa.

Dalai Lama—The title given to the head of the Tibetan monastic school dGe-lugs-pa. It translates as "Ocean (of Wisdom) Lama."

Dharma (Sanskrit)—The doctrine discovered and preached by the Buddha. It is the second of the Three Jewels of Buddhism.

Dhyana (Sanskrit)—Buddhist meditation exercises for concentrating the mind. They lead to states of mental and physical senses of ease, clarity and tranquility.

Eightfold Path—Buddha's answer to the way to eliminate desire: through correct view, correct mental attitude, correct speech, correct action, correct pursuits, correct effort, correct mindfulness and correct contemplation.

Four Noble Truths—The four doctrines taught by the Buddha as the ultimate truths of human existence. They are: life is suffering; suffering is caused by egocentric desire; suffering can be terminated through the elimination of desire; the eightfold path is the way to eliminate desire.

Fugen (Japanese)—See Samantabhadra.

Guanyin (Chinese)—Guanyin is fundamentally Avalokitesvara, the bodhisattva of goodness and compassion. However, during the 10th century Guanyin began to absorb elements from Chinese popular religion. Today, in China, Guanyin is often depicted in a female form and is associated closely with fertility as well as compassion.

Hinayana (Sanskrit)—"the lesser vehicle": the Mahayana term for all the older forms of Buddhism of which only Theravada exists today. The term is considered offensive by Theravadans.

Jataka (Sanskrit)—Stories about the former lives of the historical Buddha.

Kami (Japanese)—Indigenous Japanese deities, usually the personification of natural phenomenon. They are associated with the Shinto religion.

Kannon (Japanese)—See Avalokitesvara.

Lama (Tibetan)—A Tibetan monk.

Lamaism—Another term for Tibetan Buddhism.

Lohan (Chinese)—See Arhat.

Lotus Sutra—A fundamental Mahayana text that became the doctrine of the Tiantai (Japanese: Tendai) sect and inspired much Chinese Buddhist sculpture and painting.

Mahayana (Sanskrit)—"the great vehicle": the form of Buddhism which spread north and east from India primarily through China, Korea and Japan. Mahayana Buddhism emphasized the role of the compassionate bodhisattva.

Mandala (Sanskrit)—A circle or a cosmic diagram which serves as an aid to meditation in Esoteric Buddhism.

Manjusri (Sanskrit; Chinese: Wenshu; Japanese: Monju)—The bodhisattva of wisdom and guardian of the sacred doctrine. He usually rides a lion.

Mantra (Sanskrit)—A ritual chant with special power or potency.

Middle Path—The path between the extremes of indulgence and asceticism which, if followed, leads to enlightenment.

Monju (Japanese)—See Manjusri.

Mudra (Sanskrit)—A ritual gesture of the hands and fingers which indicates the ritual speech or action of a deity. It is used during meditation as a symbolic seal of approval from the particular deity worshipped.

Naga (Sanskrit)—Water serpent spirits.

Nat (Burmese)—A Burmese god, or powerful guardian spirit.

Nembutsu (Japanese)—The formula of faith in Pure Land Buddhism. It refers to the practice of repeating the name of Amida Buddha to insure rebirth in his Western Paradise.

Nirvana (Sanskrit)—The extinguishing of the passions of desire which leads to escape from the endless cycle of birth and death, the ultimate goal of Buddhism. The term also can refer to the physical death of an enlightened being.

Pali—Canonical language of Theravadan Buddhism. The term originally meant text.

Raigo (Japanese)—Rai means "to come" in Japanese. The term refers to a pictorial or sculptural representation of the coming of the Buddha to this world to welcome the faithful on their deathbed.

Sakyamuni (Sanskrit)—"The Sakyan sage" was a name given to the historical Buddha, Gautama.

Samantabhadra (Sanskrit; Japanese: Fugen)—The bodhisattva who embodies goodness and protects devotees of the *Lotus Sutra.* He usually rides a white elephant.

Sangha (Sanskrit)—The order of ordained monks, nuns and novices. The third of the Three Jewels of Buddhism.

Shinto (Japanese)—"Way of the Gods." Pre-Buddhist religion of Japan which expressed a reverence for nature.

Stupa (Sanskrit)—Originally it simply meant a burial mound. In Buddhist vocabulary it refers to a mound containing relics of the Buddha or of some other holy figure that is worshipped as a monument to that figure.

Sutra (Sanskrit)—A Buddhist scripture, usually one dealing with doctrine.

Tanka (Tibetan)—Ritual paintings used as aids to meditation.

Tantras (Sanskrit)—Texts added to the Mahayana canon in India in the 5th century A.D. They are manuals that describe spells, formulas, iconography and rites.

Tantric Buddhism—A form of Buddhism which combines meditation with elaborate rituals as a means towards achieving magical power and salvation.

Ten Precepts—The Buddhist vows not to kill, steal, be unchaste, lie, take intoxicants, eat at forbidden times, dance, sing or make music, use artificial adornments, use a high broad bed or receive gold or silver.

Theravada (Sanskrit)—"the Doctrine of the Elders." The form of Buddhism based upon the Pali canon that emphasizes the achievement of enlightenment by each man through his own efforts. It exists today in Ceylon (Sri Lanka), Burma, Thailand, Laos and Cambodia.

Three Jewels—The three principal elements of Buddhism: the Buddha, the Dharma, and the Sangha.

Vajra (Sanskrit)—The "thunderbolt/diamond" is a symbol of the emptiness of the world of appearances.

Vedas (Sanskrit)—A body of four religious texts composed in Sanskrit by the Aryans during the first millennium B.C.